There's No More Dying Then

There's No More Dying Then

Words of comfort and illumination

compiled by

Stephanie Wilson

SHEPHEARD-WALWYN (PUBLISHERS) LTD

First published in 2007 by
Shepheard-Walwyn (Publishers) Ltd
15 Alder Road
London SW14 8ER

British Library Cataloguing in Publication Data
A catalogue record of this book
is available from the British Library

ISBN-13: 978-0-85683-252-9
ISBN-10: 0-85683-252-9

Typeset by Alacrity, Chesterfield, Sandford, Somerset
Printed and bound in the United Kingdom
by 4edge Limited

Contents

To Diana,
whose interest in this work
was so supportive

Foreword

A LIFE'S WORK as tutor, guide and friend, has brought me into the presence of many people who were close to death. In almost every case the experience seemed to be the same: they were delightfully free and light, sometimes eager, waiting for the final call. From what I saw, there would seem to be some common features and definite stages to this transition. After one specific occasion when complete bliss surrounded the dying man, I was left, still bound in the body, with the question: just what have the philosophers across the ages actually said about death and the processes of dying?

In this brilliant piece of work, Dr Stephanie Wilson gathers together a wide spectrum of wise words from some of the world's leading philosophic and theological authorities on the topic. The purpose is not only to give hope and encouragement to the dying and their friends and families but fundamentally to remove the fear of what is inevitable for all of us. We should not wait until death is imminent: the only time to meet the reality of death is whilst we are alive. Those who have spent a good proportion of their lives studying philosophy or following a spiritual discipline seem to be better prepared for this transition. If we could really hear what these sages of humankind have to say, we could transcend death altogether and meet what they descibe as 'eternal life'.

I am so grateful to Dr Wilson for providing a source of inspiration. I am hopeful it will inspire many others.

DAVID BODDY

Introduction

WHY DID IT seem necessary to write this book?

Perhaps this question may be answered in part by considering some steps of the journey of my own faith. In later years this journey led to wide reading of the words of the wise, and studying such literature has contributed to the falling away of difficulties and fears over the prospect of death. It seemed possible that there might be a way of presenting some of this wisdom so that others could benefit from it too.

I was baptised into the Church of England in a family where going to church on a Sunday was a regular but unpressured occurrence, which was a useful start. Bible stories became very familiar and much loved, so as a child I readily accepted Christian teaching.

At school, good teaching of 'Scripture' allowed my understanding to grow, and in due course I was confirmed into the Church of England; Christianity was seen as a good thing, and at this time I was certain that God existed. Inner wonder at the glory of a tree, and the marvel of the combining power of atoms to form molecules, for instance water being formed from one atom of oxygen and two of hydrogen, re-affirmed my faith: there had to be a God who could provide such beauty, order and reason.

After six years at medical school, during the early years as a junior hospital doctor, doubts started to arise, my faith wavered. Christianity was no longer the guide that it had once been; it did not answer fundamental questions such as 'Who am I?' 'Why are we here?'

My chosen career in medicine was pathology and there were hectic years of hard work and study leading eventually to some expertise in the speciality of histopathology. This was largely diagnostic work, dealing with operation specimens and providing essential information for surgeons, skin specialists and other doctors who had taken biopsies from patients. The approach to such work was akin to that of a detective, asking questions: 'What is going on here?' 'What is behind this?' 'Why has this happened?' The other part of the work was the performing of autopsies, which are also enquiries into what and why. I began to realise that there was much more to death than its physical reality. The vitality, the personality, the soul had departed from the body, but where had it gone? I knew that only the body died. The living part of the person could no longer be in the body, but it must be somewhere. This professional work slowly helped to bring about a change in my approach to matters spiritual, reason allowed faith to return. A humanist colleague at that time could not understand how anyone doing such work could possibly believe in God; in fact the reverse was true; it would have been hard to do the work without some acknowledgement of God's existence.

Another major factor in this personal journey was my introduction to some eastern philosophical and religious thought. This exploration began to shed new light on what faith is, and to illuminate what I already knew about Christianity. I returned to study of the Bible. It also led to my beginning to learn Sanskrit, the ancient Indian language in which a vast array of important spiritual, legal, medical and other works are written. These include the *Upanishads* and the *Bhagavad Gita*. I still pursue these studies with much interest and delight.

For some years I combined a busy professional life with various aspects of spiritual study until the need to look more seriously at the topic of what death really is emerged after my 60th birthday. It became clear to me that although my particular body is not immortal, my soul and part of the mind might well be.

Then as my 70th birthday approached, and while certainties were quietly growing in my own mind, it was disconcerting to discover that crises of faith can exist even after a lifetime of belief. The younger of two sisters aged 103 and 99 fell and broke her hip. These sisters' life-long faith and spiritual nourishment in the teachings of the Church of England were severely shaken when incapacity and death seemed imminent. Fortunately for them the shock passed fairly soon but I, who knew them well, was left wondering: how common is such a loss of faith and is it really caused by the fear of death?

Shortly after this, late in 1999, I attended a lecture concerned with the challenges and needs of the coming century, and a particular challenge from the lecturer caught my attention. It was that something needed to be done about the fear of death currently to be found in British society. So I made an appointment to see the lecturer, and the outcome of that meeting eventually led to this book being researched and compiled.

The first move was to try to find out what attitudes to death other than my own were current.

There is fear in some of those who are dying, and there is also fear in some of those close to the dying. Nowadays most of us in the West have not had the frequent contact with death that our ancestors had, so we are not used to the natural sequence of birth and death. Infant mortality was very much higher in these islands in the past, but now, happily, epidemics of diseases such as diphtheria no longer make death a sadly familiar feature of childhood and young adulthood. Unfamiliarity with the cycle of birth and death can thus, of itself, cause many to fear.

For some the fear is of leaving people and things dear to them in this life. Others fear possible extinction or everlasting punishment. Attachment to the physical form can cause great grief in some of the bereaved, which can amount to fear. Some of us simply fear the unknown. There must be many variations on the simple statement 'fear of death', not least when the fears are vague. Whatever its nature, fear of death is prevalent, and it can have real power.

Having discovered all this from a variety of sources, my next move was to go back to my earlier studies to find out what the wise had written about death over the centuries. Although there are hundreds of possible sources of wisdom on this subject, reason told me that those chosen for this book ought to span many centuries and include a range of cultures. The books that had already come my way and were therefore reasonably familiar to me, were the Bible, Plato, Shakespeare, some Sanskrit texts from India, Hermes Trismegistus from Egypt, the extensive correspondence of Marsilio Ficino, priest and neo-platonist in the 15th century AD, and most recently the words of Shri Shantanada Saraswati, the Shankaracharya of the North in India and a teacher of the Vedantic tradition in the 20th century.

The effect on me of further exploration of the words of the wise opened the heart and brought light to my mind. All the texts appeared to be saying much the same things although in slightly different ways and scattered over about 3,000 years. In one year's search of these sources such profound wisdom was discovered that it was clearly time to share what I had already found rather than to continue to widen the exploration of the literature.

The next challenge was to find some way of arranging this wonderful material into a form which others could easily consider, and I spent many months trying possible methods of presentation. This was a time of quiet self-discovery, of realising that such an important matter could not be dealt

with by technical tricks. I gradually realised the necessity of
seeing what actually arose in my own mind when death was
considered as something that might well be met quite soon.
The wise have so much to say about death that is positive and
sustaining to the spirit that there should be no need to fear.
Yet I had questions, and in the end these were the key my
mind needed for me to take the next step.

In time, and it took a long time, I learned to contemplate
death in the light of this treasure house of quotations. For
contemplation to occur the mind needs to become very still,
which is not easy to achieve. In due course, and helped by
discussions, the form of the book began to take shape using
the quotations to answer the questions. The many initial
questions gradually resolved into six, and these now head the
first six chapters of the book. From my point of view these are
questions that demand to be considered and illuminated by
the words of the wise. In finding out what has been said over
the centuries on death in religious writings and in the words
of philosophers, my faith has developed with certain knowledge that a human being is not the body, nor a function such
as woman, doctor, aspirant philosopher, but a child of God,
an immortal soul based temporarily in a physical body. If one
has the opportunity to approach death steadily before undue
physical distress develops (and this can apply to all of us at
some stage, whatever may come later), study and reflection
do help. The use of texts such as these, and many more that
could have been chosen, can change or displace all sorts of
erroneous and uncomfortable ideas that may have been
harboured in the mind for a long time. That can happen; for
me it has.

How this book may be used

THIS BOOK has been compiled to help to dispel the power
of the fear of death. The quotations used contain something

of the breadth and depth of knowledge that the wise, over the centuries, have uncovered concerning many aspects of death. They answer questions frequently asked by anyone facing death, either their own death or that of others, whether full of fear or not. The questions fall into six main groups. The quotations are presented to address these six questions, one question heading each of the first six chapters. It is possible to read this book straight through as a single narrative allowing the reasonableness underlying the quotations to unfold. Particular passages can then be returned to, and perhaps reflected on.

Since fears about death vary so much and are often unspoken to anyone, and indeed are only partially admitted to ourselves, there may be some extracts, and even some chapters, that will at first be too painful to read. Perhaps they touch on something that has been disturbing the mind or heart, or both, for a long time. If that is so, it may be helpful to look at the chapter headings to see what question can be considered first.

Some may wish to face that most difficult personal fear immediately, and may then discover that the wise have already pondered the same problem over the centuries. We are not alone; the wise, by seeing the unchanging truth, offer help that varies in presentation but not in essence. Once the major fear has been looked at, other worries can then be read about with increasing recognition. These quotations, illustrating what has been said about common fears, can open up the mind to the light of reason and love, and thus help to dissolve the power of the particular fear.

This book could also be used to follow the words of a specific wise man or source. In addition, the final chapter may go some way towards the needs of those who are bereaved.

The last section includes notes on sources, giving background information about the chosen quotations, and also some reasons for including them. This is followed by a glossary indicating the way in which certain words have been used. References are listed at the back of the book so one could perhaps look at the Christian quotations and come to appreciate the amazing similarities of thought which others have expressed.

It should also be made clear that this study is directed towards mind and spirit, by bringing together statements of wisdom about death from the writings of the wise; it specifically does not address directly any physical problems to do with death.

Chapter 1

What does death mean to us, and need we fear it?

- Have you ever considered death?
- Do you fear it? Or is it something locked away in a cupboard?
- Does it make you wonder who you are?
- Is it a good idea to think about death?
- If so, should I start thinking about it now while still reasonably fit and healthy?
- Is this book necessary?
- Can such a book be helpful?

MANY OF US might immediately say 'No' to all those questions. But think for a moment: in the West today when a loved one dies we generally regard it as a tragedy whatever the age or circumstances of that person. We see it as something final even if the presence of a soul is acknowledged, and this sense of finality can generate fear – is it the end? As it is a time of heightened awareness for all, the grip of fear can be very powerful, sweeping away reason and leaving many of us apparently unable to deal with the effects.

1

Fear is always to do with loss in some way, and fear of loss of life of the body may be the greatest fear, but fear depends on our perceptions. There is an ancient story which illustrates this. Walking in the dark someone stepped on a rope, and, thinking that it was a snake, trembled with fear. He then realised that it was only a rope and not a snake, and the fear instantly evaporated.

The purpose of this book is to suggest that death is not a snake but a rope. So if any of us have a difficulty with the idea of death, where can we look for help in getting rid of the snake? Throughout history there have been some whom we may call 'the wise', who have taken a view of death that is different from many current perceptions. Realising that it is the inevitable end of any body born into this world, and that there is more to the human being than the body, the wise have faced the question and have come to see death as a moment when the real person within the body is able to escape from physical limitations and to return to the source of their being, the supreme being, God.

An exploration of some of these words of the wise has revealed much that is helpful.

There is remarkable agreement among the wise about how positive an experience this feared event can be, and this agreement among different traditions over the centuries is of itself most reassuring and of comfort. The reading of the literature from which these quotations have been selected during a long period of study, and particularly the passages chosen, has gradually shone light on the whole subject. Previously, in spite of contact with death in a professional capacity, little attention had really been given to the spiritual aspects of death; this study has been a personal revelation and is well worth sharing.

To start then with the question: What is death?

—I—

St Paul tells us:

Now if we be dead with Christ, we believe that we shall also live with Him: knowing that Christ being raised from the dead dieth no more; death hath no more dominion over him.
(*Epistle to the Romans* Ch 6 vv 8-9)

St Paul is confident in the view that not only can he believe, but all could believe that life with Christ the Son of God is what lies ahead. Paul goes on to speak of being '… **dead indeed unto sin but alive unto God** …' (*Epistle to the Romans* Ch 6 v 11). Death's power over Christ and over His followers has gone, and has been defeated.

Shakespeare also knew about this defeating. He tells us triumphantly at the end of a sonnet: '**And Death once dead, there's no more dying then**' (*Sonnet* 146). It is from this beautiful statement that the title for this book has been taken.

This change to the body can be seen as part of the unreality of the ever changing universe, something that cannot prevail against the constancy of the Eternal. Seeing this leaves open the possibility, as St Paul suggests, of life with Christ, our recognition of unity with God.

—II—

Others, who do not regard Christ in quite the same way, or who lived before His Incarnation, also speak of union with God when the Spirit leaves the body. For instance the twentieth century teacher of the ancient Vedantic scriptures, His Holiness Shri Shantananda Saraswati, the Shankaracharya of Jyoti Math in India, is also clear that it is not the end:

When a person dies, that person is going back to the Father, and it is a moment of rejoicing rather than of sorrow, because he is

attaining the ultimate state ... we should happily allow that
person to go ...   (*Birth and Death* 1993)

The change from living in this world with the limitations of
bodily infirmity, of poverty, war, etc, to the freedom of union
with the Father is very great. At whatever age it comes to that
body, at that time the real person, the soul who has lived in
that body, can return to be at one with God.

   Recall the words of Jesus: '**I and My Father are One**' (*St John*
Ch 10 v 30). We too are children of God, if we choose to
acknowledge that and merge with the Father.

—III—

What is death? In Egypt, probably at the time of Moses,
Hermes Trismegistus affirmed:

**... Death is not the destruction of what has been put together
but the dissolution of the union ... People call transformation
death, because the body is dissolved, but in fact life withdraws
into the unmanifest ...**   (*The Way of Hermes* XI.14-15)

Here Hermes is almost turning upside down many current
views on this matter. He speaks simply of the dissolution of
the attachment, the bond that a human being forges between
his physical body and the vitality within it – the Spirit that
animates that body and gives it consciousness and life.

   This animating Spirit is the breath of life described in the
creation story in the Bible:

**And the Lord God formed man of the dust of the ground, and
breathed into his nostrils the breath of life; and man became a
living soul.**   (*Genesis* Ch 2 v 7)

That same Spirit also brought life to the bones in Ezekiel's
story of the dry bones in the wilderness which were instructed

to re-unite to make human beings again (*Ezekiel* Ch 37 vv 1-10).
These bones came together and were reassembled as bodies,
but life was breathed into them by means of the Word of God.
With that breath, the living souls came too.

These days, the union between body and soul, even if
the soul is valued, often includes identification of the two.
Hermes states that at death the breath of God, the Spirit, is
withdrawn from our bodies, that is all; the union of body and
Spirit is dissolved. Then the body breaks down to be returned
to the earth, and the Spirit becomes free to soar back to the
unmanifest and to God. This is the transformation that, while
it may make us apprehensive, is truly union with God.

—IV—

Another way of considering that the end of life leads to union
with God is even older in origin:

**As from a fire fully ablaze, fly off sparks in their thousands that
are akin to the fire, similarly ... from the Imperishable originate
different kinds of creatures and into It again they merge.**

(*Mundaka Upanishad* II.i.1)

This ancient Sanskrit text also speaks of the animation of the
physical body by the Divine. It likens God, the Absolute
power, including the Imperishable Creative Force, to a
blazing fire from which sparks fly, and it says that those sparks
are what really constitute us creatures. The vital force that
ensures that our physical bodies breathe and live, is a spark
from God. When the body dies, that spark does not die down
and become extinguished, it returns to merge with the
eternal flame from which it came. This is not our usual view,
but from this viewpoint there can be nothing to fear. The
inner vitality, or essence, or soul can then be released from
the various limits that our particular physical bodies impose,
and then, when the ego has been persuaded to drop the desire

to be embodied as a separate individual, the soul can then be free to return to God.

—V—

Use of reason can influence our thoughts about what happens at the apparent end of life, as Plato teaches in the following passage; he first addresses what causes fear:

> ... if now ... God orders me to fulfil the philosopher's mission of searching into myself and other men, I were to desert my post through fear of death, or any other fear; that would indeed be strange, and I might justly be arraigned in court for denying the existence of the gods, if I disobeyed the oracle because I was afraid of death, fancying that I was wise when I was not wise. For the fear of death is indeed the pretence of wisdom, and not real wisdom, being a pretence of knowing the unknown; and no-one knows whether death, which men in their fear apprehend to be the greatest evil, may not be the greatest good. Is not this ignorance of a disgraceful sort, the ignorance of which is the conceit that man knows what he does not know? ... (*Apology* 29)

Plato is here talking about the fear that comes from our incorrect assumptions about what is evil and what is good. But, he says, because we cannot know with certainty, it is unreasonable to think that we can make a judgement on it at all. He is bringing reason to bear upon the matter, showing how a reasonable approach can be used to dispel that which is unreasonable. It is ignorant to fear something that might well be good. Death is inextricably part of life, and although we might see it like that when it is coming to others, it may be a real shock when we eventually see it coming towards ourselves. So fear is a thing we could usefully view objectively if we can, as Plato suggests.

Since it may well be the greatest good, Plato advises us to avoid 'the conceit that man knows what he does not know ...'

a point that Sherlock Holmes might have supported – he suggested that we should not theorise beyond our data.

Reason can thus steady the discursive mind where fear dwells. For some, that stilling of the mind may be sufficient to lose the fear altogether, while for others it may be the prelude to hearing with both ears, as for the first time, the words of Jesus:

Let not your heart be troubled: ye believe in God, believe also
in me.
In my Father's house are many mansions: if it were not so, I
would have told you.
I go to prepare a place for you. And if I go to prepare a place for
you, I will come again, and receive you unto myself; that where
I am, there ye may be also.'   (St John Ch 14 vv 1-3)

This is a statement about faith. Reason combined with faith brings peace to the soul, letting us see that there can be victory and ultimately union with God.

—VI—

In the Bible, victory at the end of the life of the body is emphasised in both Old and New Testaments.

St Paul writes:

... We shall all be changed in a moment, in the twinkling of an eye, at the last trump: for the trumpet shall sound, and the dead shall be raised incorruptible, and we shall be changed. For this corruptible must put on incorruption, and this mortal must put on immortality. So when this corruptible shall have put on incorruption and this mortal shall have put on immortality, then shall be brought to pass the saying that is written: Death is swallowed up in victory.'   (First Epistle to the Corinthians Ch 15 vv 51-54)

St Paul picks up a quotation from *Isaiah* (Ch 25 v 8) that God will swallow up death in victory, and speaks of dramatic change occurring very quickly, in the twinkling of an eye, the time it takes to blink once. He knew about instant change of heart because it had happened to him when he was struck blind on the road to Damascus. That blinding was by the light from heaven that accompanied the reproof that Jesus gave him for persecuting Christians. Paul's whole way of perceiving the worlds of body, mind and Spirit had been altered; his life changed within a moment, by that light, and from it he grew in faith to fulfil his true function.

The same light is also spoken of earlier in time in another tradition:

The Light even of lights, That is said to be beyond darkness; Knowledge, the Knowable, the Goal of knowledge, [It] is implanted in the heart of everyone. (*Bhagavad Gita* Ch 13 v 17)

That light which can change a life is implanted in each of us although it is usually well hidden, so well hidden that it may have to be made to manifest dramatically, as happened to St Paul. Such an experience might happen to us, but more often we have to work hard at change, digging the soil and applying compost to the garden before the roses can safely be planted, and long before there are any flowers. Gardening takes time and hard work, but the change will come; the derelict site can become a garden of tranquillity and joy. Similarly by recognition of the light a new state can prevail, and in that light the victory that St Paul speaks of can overcome all.

—VII—

St Paul's inspiration given above came from the Old Testament:

He will swallow death in victory; and the Lord God will wipe away tears from off all faces ... (*Isaiah* Ch 25 v 8)

So the final ending is not that which some expect and many fear. Many scriptural writers speak of victory at this time and of the joy that will result from this, as Isaiah does here.

Another Old Testament prophet, Hosea, quotes God as saying:

... O death, I will be thy plagues; O grave, I will be thy destruction ...   (*Hosea* Ch 13 v 14)

To Hosea also, the victory was certain.

The writer of *First Chronicles* states:

Thine, O Lord, is the greatness, and the power, and the glory, and the victory, and the majesty: for all that is in the heaven and in the earth is thine; thine is the kingdom, O Lord, and thou art exalted as head above all.   (*First Chronicles* Ch 29 v 11)

So, after the Lord's life-giving victory it is to that kingdom that we are invited – if we will accept the invitation to become one with God.

Chapter 2

Is there a heaven,
and if so what might it be like?

SOMETIMES there is a question about the destination or location of the loved one. Could it be heaven, or even hell?

Let us look first at heaven.

The word heaven conjures up a multitude of images, probably different for everyone, from playing a harp on a cloud to a bereaved mother hoping for reunion with her baby who died seventy years ago, and many more. The wise do not speak in quite such earthly images, but do use a variety of words to indicate the return of the soul to home, or to source, to rest, or to the kingdom of God, to immortality, to light, or to union, and so on. There is a wide range of imagery.

The following quotations reveal aspects of some of these words and the way they are used in reflecting the possible destination of the soul once it has left the earthly body.

—I—

First a connection with the quotation from *Chronicles* at the end of the previous chapter, where the writer has spoken of heaven and of the kingdom belonging to the Lord.

But rather seek ye the kingdom of God ... Fear not, little flock;

for it is your Father's good pleasure to give you the kingdom.
>   (*St Luke* Ch 12 vv 31-32)

Again:

... come ye blessed of my Father, inherit the kingdom prepared
for you from the foundation of the world.
>   (*St Matthew* Ch 25 v 34)

St Paul wrote:

Giving thanks unto the Father, which hath made us meet to be
partakers of the inheritance of the saints in light: Who hath
delivered us from the power of darkness, and hath translated us
into the kingdom of his dear Son.   (*Colossians* Ch 1 vv 12-13)

These writers are all telling us of heaven as the kingdom of
God, the place where we belong, where there is no darkness,
and to which we may go when we die, if we choose, or
possibly sooner. So, if we seek that kingdom, perhaps by
following the instructions of Jesus, we could then be reunited
in God and with God, even during this earthly life, before the
fall of the body.

—II—

Marsilio Ficino, priest and philosopher in fifteenth century
Florence, also uses the analogy of the kingdom, and in a
letter describing the characteristics of a philosopher, he draws
on the advice of Plato as a pathway to that kingdom:

... In the first place, he [a philosopher] is willing and prepared
to enter upon all manner of disciplines; thereafter he is truthful
by nature, completely opposed to all falsehood; in the third place
that, having scorned all that is subject to corruption, he directs
his mind to that which remains always the same. He must be

magnanimous and courageous, so that he neither fears death nor longs for empty glory.   (*Letters* 3.18)

And a little later in the same letter Ficino adds:

According to Plato, the minds of those practising philosophy having recovered their wings through wisdom and justice, as soon as they have left the body, fly back to the heavenly kingdom.

Plato, Ficino tells us, is encouraging us to take a philosophical approach to dying; we should not allow fear to be entertained by the mind. What is needed is that by practising wisdom and justice our souls may regain the wings that will permit them to fly back to God's kingdom. As the psalmist tells us: **'Thy kingdom is an everlasting kingdom'** (*Psalm* 145 v 13).

This kingdom is our natural home, from where we may, perhaps, merge with God's glory, the source of our being.

—III—

In another letter Ficino speaks of home, our homeland, which is also an expression used for the everlasting:

Since man's heavenly Father has ordained that our homeland will be heaven, we can never be content while we dwell on earth, a region far removed from our homeland … Even so the souls of men, by a common, natural impulse continually seek heaven, whence they are created, and the King of heaven beyond. But since the natural desire for God, instilled in us by God ought not to be unfulfilled (otherwise supreme reason, which does nothing in vain, has bestowed it upon us in vain), it follows that the souls of men are eternal, in order that one day they may be able to reach the eternal, divine good which their nature desires.
                                                            (*Letters* 3.4)

Part of the divine good spoken of here is happiness, true bliss. Every one of us desires happiness. For one person, like Shaw's Eliza Doolittle, this might include a box of chocolates, to another it might be a proposal of marriage or marriage itself. But what needs to be realised is that such things are not eternal. Happiness is an aspect of God, and supreme happiness only comes by being with God, or in God. Ficino thus speaks of 'our homeland', heaven, that place, that state beyond which may be found the king of heaven. It is also the place which was:

Before the mountains were brought forth or ever thou hadst formed the earth and the world even from everlasting to everlasting ...   *(Psalm* 90 v 2)

This is where we find eternal bliss, in this life as well as the next.

—IV—

What about the eternal aspect of heaven, of eternity?
    The word 'eternity' is used by Shakespeare.

**... All that lives must die,
Passing through nature to eternity.**   *(Hamlet* Act I sc ii)

... and make us heirs of all eternity.   *(Love's Labours Lost* Act I sc i)

Shakespeare wrote widely on life and death, expressed through characters taking different points of view. Hamlet's mother, Gertrude, is a lady much involved with the senses and the physical body. Yet she is able to tell Hamlet, who is grieving for his dead father, about eternity. She knows that all who are born must eventually die, and that whatever is living is merely on a journey through nature, through an ephemeral life on this earth to something that is truly durable.

Likewise the young king in *Love's Labours Lost*, who, in laying out his scheme of a perfect philosophical life, tells his friends that in due course, time will release them (and us) from this life and its ills, to inherit eternity.

And Jesus said:

My sheep hear my voice, and I know them, and they follow me. And I give unto them eternal life; and they shall never perish, neither shall any man pluck them out of my hand.

(*St John* Ch 10 vv 27-28)

So eternity is indicating our true 'home' to which we may return and then merge with God – if we so wish.

—V—

The divine world is sometimes equated with heaven, so how has the word 'divine' been used?

Marsilio Ficino describes 'divine music'. He writes that the followers of Plato say that one kind of divine music

… exists entirely in the eternal mind of God. The second [kind of divine music] is in the motions and order of the heavens, by which the heavenly spheres and their orbits make a marvellous harmony. In both of these our soul took part before it was imprisoned in our bodies … The whole soul then kindles with desire to fly back to its rightful home, so that it may enjoy that true music again. It realises that as long as it is enclosed in the dark abode of the body, it can in no way reach that music …

(*Letters* 1.7)

Ficino tells us of the expansion of experience that can be appreciated and understood when the true living being, the essence within each of us, the soul, is freed from the limitations of the body. We have all had brief tastes of this unlimited freedom of being truly in touch with God, even though we might not call it that. Sometimes the word liberation is used in this connection.

Shri Shantananda Saraswati says:

Taking a body or leaving the body has no relation to liberation. The liberation is to understand that I am not the body, and once this is achieved one is liberated of all bonds ... (*Birth and Death* 1993)

Let us consider that if we were to lose our physical bonds and cease to be enclosed by our bodies, then perhaps we could recognise that before we are born and after we die we can be free in the company of that divine harmony; that harmony which is an integral part of God and is therefore our rightful and natural home where we can rejoin the being of God.

—VI—

The word divine was also important in much earlier times. In the *Bhagavad Gita*, the Lord Krishna speaks to Prince Arjuna about a good life, and makes this statement:

Surely wisdom is like the sun, revealing the supreme truth to those whose ignorance is dispelled by the wisdom of the Self. Meditating on the Divine, having faith in the Divine, concentrating on the Divine, and losing themselves in the Divine ... they go where there is no return.   (*Bhagavad Gita* Ch 5 vv 16-17)

Usually these days we do not consider that we have the divine within us, but identify ourselves with the physical body. We tend to define ourselves in terms of our looks, good or bad, or our shape, and so on, often taking much less account of the mind within, although the mind, like the body, may also be helping to hide our souls and true essence. But by turning to the divine, help is available. Krishna's sense of the divine is echoed by Marsilio Ficino who writes of the possibility of seeing:

... through to the inner man, to his very soul, which being given from God to man is immortal and divine. (*Letters* 1.111)

We worry so much about what happens to our bodies when we die, yet the body will disperse to the elements eventually in one way or another. What is more important is what happens to the '**inner man**' that Ficino describes. So what is this inner man? Who is he? Could we relate it to ourselves and say: 'What is the inner man in me?' or perhaps: 'Who am I?'

That inner man, the soul, is the spark within, the essence of each of us that is immortal and divine, and that may be what is meant when the Bible tells us that we are made in the image of God (*Genesis* 1 vv 26-27). So when the body falls, that which is divine within us can return to lose itself in the Divine, that is, to attain to everlasting union with the Supreme Being.

Chapter 3

How can we learn
to face the fear of death?

AS THE WISE encourage a more positive attitude towards
the end of our earthly existence, speaking of freedom
from limitations of the body, a more blessed state,
why then is fear so prevalent at this time?

One possible factor is the word hell. What this word
conjures up varies in different traditions and cultures, and
probably has many shades of meaning, differing in individual
people. The word has an uncomfortable quality about it, even
when it is merely taken to mean the place of the dead, which
seems to be generally so in the Old Testament of the Bible.
But it can have a terrifying feel to it, and this has been
nurtured in various Christian traditions over the centuries.
The belief in a place of punishment for the personal soul,
overseen by some higher authority, was apparent in the ethos
of burning martyrs at various times in England, or in the
activities of the Spanish Inquisition.

Does the idea of hell provoke that recurring question of
who am I? Is there a lingering doubt, half hidden at the back
of the mind, only occasionally being allowed to surface, that
hell is one of the possible outcomes that lies ahead for a
person such as me? If one is unsure who one is, if doubt has
been allowed to creep in, then fear could easily prevail.

So what light comes from the wise on this concept? Perhaps most of us do not often turn our minds to the fairly small number of passages in the gospels where Jesus mentions hell. These make uneasy reading, for we may not have a full understanding of what His meaning is.

—I—

Both St Matthew (in Chapter 10) and St Luke record a similar, quite long passage. St Luke's account contains these words:

And I say unto you my friends, be not afraid of them that kill the body, and after that they have no more that they can do. But I will forewarn you whom ye shall fear. Fear him, which after he hath killed hath power to cast into hell; yea, I say unto you, fear him.   (*St Luke* Ch 12 vv 4-5)

This sounds frightening, and the mind might want to hide away from such words. But as with so many sayings of Jesus, the question needs to be asked: What does He mean?

It is certainly possible to consider that this and other such statements are a condemnation, not of our souls, but of the selfish part of our beings, our egos. It is the ego, constructed as it is of personal desires, that can beguile and try to overwhelm the true Self and lead the way to misery. So it is the ego that should be cast aside. We may know in our hearts what is the right thing to do, but we are often too timid to contradict the ego. To clarify this matter the very next words of Jesus in this passage from St Luke are of hope and peace:

Are not five sparrows sold for two farthings, and not one of them is forgotten before God? ... Fear not therefore, ye are of more value than many sparrows.   (*St Luke* Ch 12 vv 6-7)

By these words Jesus seems to suggest that there is no inevitability of our souls being cast away anywhere.

A similar view, setting out a path to hell is laid out step by step by the Lord Krishna:

When a man thinks of objects, attachment for them arises. From attachment arises desire; from desire arises wrath. From wrath arises delusion; from delusion, failure of memory; from failure of memory, loss of conscience; from loss of conscience he is utterly ruined.   (*Bhagavad Gita* Ch 2 vv 62-63)

As with the quotation from St Luke, this disturbing statement by Krishna is followed by words of deliverance from the grim sequence described, and he provides practical advice as to how to find peace and tranquillity.

In peace there is an end of all his miseries; for the reason of the tranquil-minded soon becomes steady.   (*Bhagavad Gita* Ch 2 v 65)

—II—

Deep grief can arise in some of us brought up as Christians but whose faith has wavered so that there is fear of the implications of the last twenty words of the following passage from St John's gospel:

For God so loved the world that He gave His only begotten Son, that whosoever believeth in Him should not perish, but have everlasting life. For God sent not His Son into the world to condemn the world; but that the world through Him might be saved. He that believeth on Him is not condemned: but he that believeth not, is condemned already, because he hath not believed in the only begotten Son of God. (*St John* Ch 3 vv 16-18)

This last sentence could easily make people afraid that they are the condemned, but the passage continues:

And this is the condemnation, that light is come into the world, and men loved darkness rather than light, because their deeds were evil. For everyone that doeth evil hateth the light, neither cometh to the light, lest his deeds should be reproved. But he that doeth truth cometh to the light, that his deeds may be made manifest, that they are wrought in God.

(St John Ch 3 vv 19-21)

We are invited to turn to the truth and thus come to the light, away from the desires of the ego, and that is the way out of hell. Frightening memories of this portrayal of hell often from long ago, may play a part in our fears. So if they do exist, they need to be looked straight in the eye. Facing up to such fears and letting them be seen in the loving context of light can help, for it is only in the present that change can come.

—III—

But there is also the question of hell on earth, what one might call a living death, when seriously unpleasant and distressing situations arise in our lives, particularly when they persist. Sometimes such things apparently come out of the blue, but sometimes we can see that we choose to separate ourselves from others and from God, and thus make our own hell on earth by the strength of our self-love, our attachments to our own private identities. If we are all children of God, or sparks from the eternal flame of God as described in the *Mundaka Upanisad* (see Chapter 1.IV), then we are also all part of a whole, and to reject another child of God or another spark from eternal light is to separate ourselves off quite deliberately into a very small world. That world will be a form of hell, which may be lonely, vindictive, guilt-ridden, or all three, and more besides.

Many psalms speak of the misery to which mankind is subjected, for instance, those that

... sit in darkness and in the shadow of death being bound in affliction and iron, because they rebelled against the words of God and contemned [sic] the counsel of the most High ... they fell down and there was none to help. (*Psalm* 107 vv 10-12)

This is dramatic language, but so often the turning away from what we know to be true and right, and forgetting and abandoning God, means that we have identified with our own physical bodies and our own private interests, and this does ultimately lead to misery and there does not seem to be any help available.

Ficino also appreciates the danger of the self-love we have for our bodies rather than our souls:

How worthy of love, how worthy of admiration is this form of the soul, whose shadow is the form of the body so loved and admired by everyone. (*Letters* 4.51)

In another letter he spells this out even more clearly:

... In the life of the body we are a prey to a host of trivial vexations. The life of the body is a penance, worthy to be called the death of the soul. (*Letters* 1.108)

Ficino is pointing out the strange way we have of looking at the relative importance of the body and the soul. We value our bodies so much, particularly when young and fit, when we can delight in physical achievement. Later on we still cling on to the worldly achievements of our individual selves, even when the body takes on burdens that can become a penance, and which in some may lead to a complete ignoring of the soul and its state of health. This is a form of hell.

We need to nourish the soul with true food for the mind culled from the scriptures and the words of the wise of many cultures. If we could recognise the pre-eminence of the soul, and just care for the body in an intelligent way without self-indulgence, then life could be much simpler, without our usual attachment to the physical body. Then as the life of the body approaches its end, it may not be so difficult to let it go, without fear.

—IV—

Darkness is another metaphor for hell on earth. Job knew about this; he was having a very hard time. With God's permission he had been persecuted by Satan in many ways to try to get him to curse God. During his prolonged ordeal he cries out to God about his troubles, and asks if they could cease and perhaps he could receive a little comfort:

… before I go whence I shall not return, even to the land of darkness and the shadow of death; a land of darkness, as darkness itself, and of the shadow of death, without any order, and where the light is as darkness.   (*Job* Ch 10 vv 21-22)

During this most distressing time in his life Job could only anticipate darkness ahead. Darkness is also an important factor in Plato's remarkable allegory of the cave (from the *Republic*), which tells of a man, brought up in the dimly lit, very restricted confines of a cave, possibly the sort of place that Job felt himself to be in. The man in the cave eventually escapes to a world of light and reality, but his introduction to the world above has to be gradual and gentle because at first he cannot bear the brightness of what he finds there.

Ficino comments on this story:

… in this world the wretched souls, shut in by the shadows and windowless prison of the deathbound body, never in fact look upon themselves, or anything else, or the real Sun but look instead upon the shadows of themselves and of other things and a faint image of the real Sun …   (*Letters* 5.48)

He then draws a parallel between Plato's story of the dismal cave contrasted with the reality shining in sunlight, and the relationship of this world that we live in and that which he calls 'invisible and divine'. He likens us to the hapless creatures reared and confined in the cave, only able to see shadows, and compelled by their egos to stay there. He warns us that it may take us a while to adjust to the idea of escape from what Shakespeare describes as '... this mortal coil ...' (*Hamlet* Act III sc i). New ideas can be hard to accept; we need to disentangle ourselves by dropping our prejudices, opinions and fears.

In Ficino's quotation we are being urged to turn away from shadows to reality, as Job eventually was able to do, and to put less emphasis on our earthly bodies and instead attend to our 'wretched souls' (as Ficino calls them) so that they can be released from prison, and then glory in their return to God.

—V—

The belief that death is the end of existence is a common view, overtly feared by some, and perhaps secretly by many, and this too can be a form of hell.

Shri Shantananda Saraswati has said:

It is the body that is born and dies. The Atman itself which inhabits the body is birthless and deathless. (*Birth and Death* 1993)

Ficino also speaks of this erroneous belief, linking it with darkness in the same letter that has been quoted earlier in chapter 3.IV.

... when the soul descends from the immense light of the invisible world into a dark body to rule and move it, it is overwhelmed by strange shadows opposed to its own nature and is compelled to suffer blindness and hallucinations for a long time

and to stagger about ... all mortals ... deserve this, since they
are foolish enough to allow themselves to be deceived into
thinking that this anxious sojourn of the heavenly and immortal
soul in the earthly realm of death is real life, although they clearly
see it beginning right at the start with omens of screams and tears
and ending in perpetual complaint and final misery. But on the
other hand, when the immortal soul, freed from the mortal body,
returns to life, they believe death is occurring. This they believe
quite wrongly, for only when recurrent death is dead does real
eternal life arise.   (*Letters* 5.48)

What a mirror of the lives of many Ficino displays here.
Some of us do live in evident misery; others put a brave face
on secret fears or deep distress. Ficino is describing what is
undoubtedly hell on earth, only too real for millions of our
fellow human beings. And the misery is compounded by the
belief that the release of the Spirit that is described in this
quotation will not come. Ficino knew what William Shakespeare expressed so well a century later:

Death once dead, there's no more dying then.   (*Sonnet* 146)

If only we could learn to turn right round with our backs
to the idea of hell and look towards truth and God, and to
see that there is no need to identify with suffering, even when
things do seem bad. Then perhaps we can learn to drop one
by one the layers of misery, and so see at last the light of God
that always shines, but which, because of the barriers of
misery, we frequently cannot see. Then maybe our inner light
can join God's light, knowing that the Spirit that inhabits the
body is both birthless and deathless, as Shri Shantananda
Saraswati tells us.

—VI—

In Plato's allegory of the cave (see Chapter 3.IV) shadows were seen to be disturbing. Another early writer was also wary of them.

The writer of *First Chronicles* centuries before, had proclaimed:

... our days on earth are as a shadow ...
(First Chronicles Ch 29 v 15)

There is no inevitability in our attraction to shadows; there is a choice:

O mind that belongs to the heavens, you love your earthly shadow – that is the body – more than the heavenly splendour, your own light, more than the light that is above the heavens.
(Letters 2.40)

Shadows are a large part of the fears about life and what may come after. Shadows are present when we turn our backs on the light of God. Light, Genesis tells us, was the first substance to become manifest in creation:

And God said, 'Let there be light': and there was light.
(Genesis Ch 1 v 3)

Shadows will be present in our lives if we ignore the true source of the light and turn away from it. But the light that is above the heavens may become available to us all, possibly in the course of this life if the choice is recognised, for it is our own light too. This recognition is more likely as life draws to a close and when enlightenment with the light of God may be both more easily responded to, and more readily appreciated.

—VII—

We have now looked at various difficulties: the fear of the possibility of hell as a state following the death of the body, the existence of hell on earth, and the fear that possibly death of the body is final.

And the matter of real choice has now been raised. To help in this choice it is necessary to seek for and accept a change of attitude. Once again the question: Who am I? is relevant.

I can only judge it the most foolish act of all, that many people most diligently feed a beast, that is their body, a wild, cruel and dangerous animal; but allow themselves, that is, the soul ... to starve to death. We are surprised that while we continue to live, or rather die like this, we are unhappy, as though we could reap a different harvest from the one we have sown. Misery is the fruit of foolishness. How is this? Because we foolishly over-feed the body and neglect the soul, the body becomes fat and robust and the soul thin and puny. So it comes about that the soul, in its meagre and feeble state, sees physical things as both large and strong. The soul greatly desires what looks large, but fears what looks strong even more. For this reason, in its misery, it is harassed partly by the passion of greed and partly by the dread of fear.   (*Letters* 1.57)

We may find this description of the state of many of us hard to believe or even – 'this can't apply to me!' but do we not tend to indulge our bodies by comfort eating or going to buy a new dress or fashion accessories of all kinds, perhaps even including a swanky car or diamond earrings? Am I perhaps the beast that Ficino describes? How often does it come to mind to step outside this hell on earth and to fall quiet and seek God's help, perhaps to read the Sermon on the Mount, or a psalm, or to reflect on the omniscience and stability of the Creator? Many fall into despair, and depression is now among the commonest of illnesses. Ficino has spelled out what we so often allow to happen. But this foolishness (as he calls it) is not necessary: '... **I know that my Redeemer liveth** ...' as Job proclaimed in time of real trouble (*Job* Ch 19 v 25).

—VIII—

So having faced up to hell in various forms, is there a way out? The wise speak of the strong bond that exists between God and us which cannot be broken if we believe. The Lord Krishna, speaking of his divinity, gives a simple instruction as to how it is possible to come to know God at the time of dying:

Whosoever at the time of death thinks only of Me, and thinking thus leaves the body and goes forth, assuredly he will know Me.
(*Bhagavad Gita* Ch 8 v 5)

And Ficino, having first specified the miserable state of mind of many, also indicates how a profound difference can come about:

Since Man, with his restless mind, feeble frame, and desire for everything, leads a harder life on earth than the very beasts, then, if nature were to appoint for him exactly the same limit of life as for other creatures, no animal could have a sadder lot than he. But it is not possible that Man, who by worship of God comes nearest of all creatures to God, the source of happiness, could be the least happy of all. Therefore it is only after the death of the body that his greater happiness may be achieved ...
(*Ficino* 1.111)

Thus there can be release from the tribulations of life – life as a human being can be one of hardship for many. It is rare for any of us to have a smooth run right through life, but although what is presented to us, however hard, gives an opportunity for something to be learnt, some of us lead the sort of earthly life that Ficino describes, which may well be considered as hell on earth. But both Krishna and Ficino know that when the body dies there can be release from all the difficulties of life, as, say, from all the limitations of life as a caterpillar – who, if only he knew, could look forward to the freedom of becoming a butterfly.

—IX—

And Jesus said:

Verily, verily, I say unto you, he that heareth my word, and believeth on him that sent me, hath everlasting life, and shall not come into condemnation; but is passed from death unto life. Verily, verily, I say unto you, 'The hour is coming and now is, when the dead shall hear the voice of the Son of God: and they that hear shall live.   (*St John* Ch 5 vv 24-25)

Years ago this seemed very puzzling. How could the dead hear the voice of God and then live? Was this talk of souls or bodies? Considering this passage now, it seems that when we have cut ourselves off from God by forgetting Him and identifying with our physical bodies or with our various functions here on earth, we are so separated from God that we can be described, not unreasonably, as dead. But Jesus points out that some people, some of us, will actually come to hear what He is really saying, if we choose to hear, and then we can be released from a homemade hell:

He that has ears to hear, let him hear.   (*St Matthew* Ch 11 v 15)

Likewise in the *Bhagavad Gita* similar advice is given by Krishna:

Fix thy mind on Me, devote thyself to Me, sacrifice for Me, surrender to Me, make Me the object of thy aspirations, and thou shalt assuredly become one with Me, who am thine own Self.

(*Bhagavad Gita* Ch 9 v 34)

Many people are unhappy nowadays for all sorts of reasons, and depression (which, as has been said, is now common) often leads to a narrow and limited view of life when it becomes hard to be in touch with reason, let alone God. With Krishna advocating complete devotion to the One Lord of all, and Jesus assuring us that we will be able to hear His words with understanding that can lead to a way out from hell on earth, then the transformation to real life and light and union with God could take place.

—X—

In earlier centuries too, it was known that there is a way out of suffering at the end of the life of the body, for instance in the psalms:

The Lord is my light and my salvation; whom shall I fear? The Lord is the strength of my life; of whom shall I be afraid?

(*Psalm* 27 v 1)

With this knowledge of the light and the strength of the Lord being available to him, it is no wonder that the psalmist was also able to say:

… God will redeem my soul from the power of the grave; for he shall receive me.   (*Psalm* 49 v 15)

This news helps to counter the idea that the power of the grave brings with it fear of separation, including fear of ceasing to be, with the feeling of rejection that can accompany this. The psalmist, by stating 'for he shall receive me', knew that any fears he may have had are rendered nonsense, and that the grave, representing the fate of the body, will not prevail. Being received by God is like being drawn back to Him as iron is attracted to a magnet. But if we cling to our own desires this cannot happen. If we choose to let the cherished desires of our egos go, we can return to God.

—XI—

Lastly in this chapter a statement of profound hope by Ficino reinforces the psalmist's knowledge: '**The blessed soul can never be removed from God**' (*Letters* 1.115).

And having made this confident statement Ficino then goes on to say that removal of the soul from God cannot be done forcibly and asks: '**Where is the force that can be inflicted on a soul enveloped in the infinite power of God?**' (*ibid*).

So who are the blessed? Jesus has said:

… **Come, ye blessed of my Father, inherit the kingdom prepared for you from the foundation of the world** …

(*St Matthew* Ch 25 v 34)

And in the Sermon on the Mount Jesus recounts a long list of those who are blessed.

Blessed are the poor in spirit: for theirs is the kingdom of heaven.
Blessed are they that mourn: for they shall be comforted.
Blessed are the meek: for they shall inherit the earth.
Blessed are they which do hunger and thirst after righteousness: for they shall be filled.
Blessed are the merciful: for they shall obtain mercy.
Blessed are the pure in heart: for they shall see God.
Blessed are the peace makers: for they shall be called the children of God.
Blessed are they which are persecuted for righteousness' sake: for theirs is the kingdom of heaven.

Blessed are ye, when men shall revile you, and persecute you, and shall say all manner of evil against you falsely, for my sake.
(*St Matthew* Ch 5 vv 3-12)

When the world began we were blessed, and still are. And Ficino concludes his beautiful statement by telling us that: '**... he who once finds happiness in God finds it forever**' (*Letters* 1.115).

For anyone who enquires into such matters, this can bring great comfort as a way out from hell, and as a signpost to God.

Chapter 4

What can we do *now*
to influence what happens
as we perceive the end
of life approaching?

H AVING LOOKED at some of the fears that the word
death provokes, we begin to realise that it can be
looked upon as a release from bondage; bondage of the
Spirit by the body, and start to realise who we really are.
Sometimes the comments of the wise seem to be telling us the
steps we might take to look into our own hearts to change
this situation with regard to what we do, with the way we look
upon ourselves, upon others, and sometimes the way we regard
the Divine. In the end, of course, these blend into one
another and there is no real difference, just a variation in
point of view.

—I—

How can we start to have a new look at ourselves? We need
to start from where we are:

**... the advantage of a human body is that you can open your
inner eye and see your true Self.** (*Birth and Death* 1993)

We are being told that there is the possibility of seeing through to the truth within us now.

This is not easy, and Marsilio Ficino offers some good advice:

Let us, I beg you, nourish and increase the spirit with spiritual food, so that it may at length become mighty and have small regard for physical things, as though they were worth very little. Then may no part of the spirit shift from its own seat through the assaults of the flesh.

Let us climb into the high watch tower of the mind, leaving the dust of the body below; then we will gaze more closely at the divine and view the mortal from a distance. The former will seem greater than usual, and the latter smaller. So, cherishing the divine, and disregarding the mortal, we will no longer be foolish or miserable, but indeed wise and happy.   (*Letters* 1.57)

Having laid before us earlier in this same letter (quoted in Chapter 3.VII) a problem widespread in this world of ours, where fears and misery are prevalent, Ficino now suggests a solution, and urges us to nourish the spirit with appropriate food, and to cherish that within us which is divine.

A change of perspective in this way is not only possible (although it may take time and requires us to remember this new approach as constantly as we can), but it is the only certain way out. Hermes, whose writings influenced Ficino, had written long before about seekers after truth:

Having thus raised themselves they see the Supreme Good, and realising that, they regard time spent here as a misfortune. Disregarding the gross and the subtle, they hasten to the One alone.   (*The Way of Hermes* IV.5)

The wise can see that there is delight at the end of earthly life.

—II—

Another way that we might help ourselves is by reading some
of Shakespeare's words. Like all the wise, he knew that the
essence of man, if permitted by the ego, can drop earthly
limits and be in touch with the Divine. For example:

SONNET 29

When, in disgrace with Fortune and men's eyes,
I all alone beweep my outcast state,
And trouble deaf heaven with my bootless cries,
And look upon myself and curse my fate,
Wishing me like to one more rich in hope,
Featur'd like him, like him with friends possess'd,
Desiring this man's art and that man's scope,
With what I most enjoy contented least;
Yet in these thoughts myself almost despising,
Haply I think on thee, and then my state,
Like to the lark at break of day arising
From sullen earth, sings hymns at heaven's gate:
For thy sweet love remember'd such wealth brings,
That then I scorn to change my state with kings.

SONNET 30

When to the sessions of sweet silent thought
I summon up remembrance of things past,
I sigh the lack of many a thing I sought,
And with old woes new wail my dear times' waste:
Then can I drown an eye, unus'd to flow,
For precious friends hid in death's dateless night,
And weep afresh love's long since cancell'd woe,
And moan the expense of many a vanish'd sight:
Then can I grieve at grievances foregone,
And heavily from woe to woe tell o'er

The sad account of fore-bemoaned moan,
Which I new pay as if not paid before.
But if the while I think on thee, dear friend,
All losses are restor'd and sorrows end.

In both of these sonnets, the poet initially sounds very sorry for himself because of the woes of the world that are afflicting his ego. This may well be the attitude we take up when the world seems against us, perhaps in old age when physical difficulties develop and the body is full of aches and pains; maybe in middle age when happiness and worldly success in a variety of ways has apparently eluded us, or at any age when disability or serious ill health come along, and most of all, perhaps, if a loved one has died, or when the end of one's own individual life appears to be in sight. At such times, to turn to things of the Spirit, to the source of light and life, can transform the whole scene – as one remembers that one true friend that Shakespeare writes about, which is the love of God that leads to the end of sorrow, bringing true wealth and happiness and finally union with the Divine.

—III—

Another useful aid that can give insight into out true nature is the use of reason:

Know yourself, offspring of God in mortal clothing. I pray you, uncover yourself. Separate the soul from the body, reason from sensual desires; separate them as much as you can; and your ability depends on your endeavour. When the earthly grime has been removed, you will at once see pure gold, and when the clouds have been dispersed, you will see the clear sky. Then believe me you will revere yourself as an eternal ray of the divine sun ...   (*Letters* 1.110)

These words resonate with:

He who is happy within his Self and has found Its peace, and in whom the inner light shines, that sage attains Eternal Bliss and becomes the Spirit Itself. (*Bhagavad Gita* Ch 5 v 24)

We are being urged to emulate the sages and to recognise who we really are, to see that we are soul as well as body, and that the soul is of the nature of the divine light of God, the Self. But it is not an easy task that is being put before us, although it is possible. We need to look very carefully at the way we behave, and what our habits are. We can't just wave a magic wand or rub a magic lamp like Aladdin's. We need to learn to allow those unhelpful habits and entrenched ideas about ourselves to drop, so that we may get rid of the '**earthly grime**'. But once these limiting ideas and thoughts are shed we will be able to see that we are indeed as eternal rays of the divine sun, and so – just as a sunbeam cannot be separated from the sun – we cannot, ultimately, be separated from God, our Source, the Supreme Self.

—IV—

What else do we need in this search for our true selves and a way forward that will help to allay any fears? Perhaps a clear vision, and to turn our attention directly to the Supreme:

Those who make Me their refuge, who strive for liberation from decay and death; they realise the Supreme Spirit, which is their own real Self ... Those who see Me in the life of the world ... as pure Divinity, keeping their minds steady, they live in Me, even in the crucial hour of death. (*Bhagavad Gita* Ch 7 vv 29-30)

This statement by the Lord Krishna can be usefully contrasted with a comment of Ficino's:

... the soul is the man himself and the body but his shadow. Whatever wretch is so deluded as to think that the shadow of man is man, like Narcissus is dissolved in tears ... (*Letters* 1.15)

Ficino tells us that we are our souls, and not our bodies nor our egos nor functions in life. Krishna has an even larger view, telling us how we, our real selves, can become one with the Supreme Spirit. If these statements can be accepted, then the fear dissolves – for it is as much a shadow as our insubstantial bodies. We get so attached to our bodies, even when they have ceased to function in the way we would like, that we have come to think that they are the real substance. Following this path leads to tears. So if we can take on board Krishna's advice as to what is true and where we should look for truth, and to consider the soul as the essence of the person, and cease to be deluded, we will know the reality about our souls and that, when this earthly life comes to an end, we can soar out of our bodies and return to God.

As the writer of *Ecclesiastes* says:

Then shall the dust return to the earth as it was; and the spirit shall return to God who gave it. (*Ecclesiastes* Ch 12 v 7)

—V—

Sometimes a direct instruction is helpful in this search for understanding, and the Old Testament can be a useful source for this kind of reminder:

... I have no pleasure in the death of him that dieth, saith the Lord God: wherefore turn yourselves, and live ye.
(*Ezekiel* Ch 18 v 32)

Here Ezekiel indicates the compassion of God in not wanting us to give in to the idea that death is the end, but instead instructs us to turn our lives round 180 degrees and to realise that what we actually face at this point is life.

Similarly, in *Deuteronomy* God is reported as saying:

... I have set before you life and death, blessing and cursing: therefore choose life ... (*Deuteronomy* Ch 30 v 19)

So what choices are being put before us? Do we choose to curse our fate as Shakespeare states in Sonnet 29 (see Chapter 4.II)? Do we choose to die with fear or many fears? Can we begin to realise who we really are and therefore prepare to die full of joy, or at least live in the prospect of imminent union with God, either at the death of the body or perhaps sooner?

—VI—

A direct question may add emphasis to an instruction.

… Why, O men born of earth, have you given yourselves over to death while having the power to partake of immortality? Repent. You who have kept company with those who have wandered and have shared in ignorance, be released from the dark light, take part in immortality … *(The Way of Hermes* 1.28)

The sage is asking us why we choose such a pessimistic view of life when this is not necessary. He speaks of dark light, an unusual phrase, but it indicates graphically that unreal world where misery and pain abound, a world we have all entered from time to time, and where many live all the time. To Hermes Trismegistus it is strange indeed that we choose to be so well acquainted with such a hell on earth when we can change our viewpoint, and, seeing things differently, take part in immortality, now, even in this earthly life. He knows without doubt that this reasonable approach would help us, if we are willing to take such a step.

—VII—

There are many qualities that can be of assistance in this enquiry, for instance steadfastness.

If a man die, shall he live again? all the days of my appointed time will I wait, till my change come. *(Job Ch 14 v 14)*

Job, as we have heard, was being persecuted by Satan, but, refusing to criticise God, Job knew in his heart and soul that a change would come if he remained steadfast and patiently waited for the Lord to release him from his misery. The waiting was not easy because of the physical and mental persecution that he was being subjected to. The psalmist also knew the value of such patience:

Our soul waiteth for the Lord: he is our help and our shield. For our heart shall rejoice in him, because we have trusted in his holy name. Let thy mercy, O Lord, be upon us according as we hope in thee.   (*Psalm* 33 vv 20-22)

St Paul valued long-suffering, listing it with other qualities of the Spirit:

But the fruit of the Spirit is love, joy, peace, long-suffering, gentleness, goodness, faith, meekness, temperance; against such there is no law.   (*Epistle to the Galations* Ch 5 vv 22-23)

So the question arises: can we wait for the change to come? Waiting can be hard; it requires patience, long-suffering and self-discipline as well as steadfastness. But if all this can come about, then Job's query **'shall he live again?'** can be answered with an unshakeable 'Yes', and reunion with God can happen.

—VIII—

In another tradition we hear of devotion being a help at this time:

There is no loss of effort here, there is no harm. Even a little of this devotion delivers one from great fear.

(*Bhagavad Gita* Ch 2 v 40)

This verse from the *Bhagavad Gita* was commented on centuries ago by Shankara, the first Shankaracharya, who said:

… there is no uncertainty regarding the result of any effort in the path of Yoga [devotion]. Neither is there any chance of harm resulting from it … Anything done, however little it be, in this path of Yoga saves one from great fear, from the fear of samsara – of birth and death.   (*Bhagavad Gita* commentary on Ch 2 v 40)

This statement has a resonance with St John, who said:

There is no fear in love; but perfect love casteth out fear …
                            (*First Epistle of St John* Ch 4 v 18).

Devotion to God with love, looking out away from our own egos, allows the view to change, and to release us from the fear that many of us have of mortality.

—IX—

And now what might we do to relieve and set to rights any unhelpful attitudes towards other people? There are two main difficulties in this context.

St John says:

We know that we have passed from death unto life, because we love the brethren. He that loveth not his brother abideth in death.   (*First Epistle of St John* Ch 3 v 14)

If we don't follow Jesus's instruction to '… **Love thy neighbour as thyself** …' (*St Mark* Ch 12 v 31) we cause great limitations and unhappiness, a hell on earth. St John speaks of loving our brothers, and the effect of not doing so. For some it is harder to love their own families than to love their friends. So, not loving can become a great burden, and can cause a great waste

of energy as we battle with guilt about it. Our view can
become so sadly limited that we can hardly see beyond our
own bodies, and 'what is good for me' is all that matters; we
just love our own egos.

So who are our brothers? Jesus said:

**... whosoever shall do the will of my Father which is in heaven,
the same is my brother, and sister, and mother ...**

(*St Matthew* Ch 12 v 50)

As it is possible for anyone to do the will of God, let us look
outwards, and give love to the brethren that St John speaks
of, whoever they may be. This giving of love may well be
shown in service to those brothers and sisters. It may then
be possible to love society, even perhaps the nation, and so
humanity, and thus pass to eternal life before the body dies.

—X—

Much private grief can come because of identifying our loved
ones with their physical bodies.

Shri Shantananda Saraswati echoing words of St John says:

**... when the love of the physical body ceases to exist, then the
real love comes ... yet it is very difficult for people to transcend
the love of the physical body, although it is equally true that
we love the physical not for the sake of the physical, but for the
sake of the Atman within the physical, but somehow we get
entangled and limit the whole thing to the physical body – then
when the pleasure of being in physical proximity is denied
then we feel sorry, but this sorrow is unnecessary – this is the
hindrance to real love.** (*Birth and Death* 1993)

We all too readily get the physical world entangled with the
spiritual world, and understand wrongly that the person we
love has died, when in truth it is the body that has been left

behind by the departing soul. It is the body that has died and this will in due course return to the earth from which it was formed. As St John says:

That which is born of the flesh is flesh; and that which is born of the Spirit is spirit.   (*St John* Ch 3 v 6)

Then the departing soul can again be one with God.

— XI —

A letter written by Marsilio Ficino to a bereaved friend, also echoes a statement from the *Bhagavad Gita:*

Tell me, Bernado, what is it that you mourn in a friend's death? Is it death? Or is it the person who is dead? If it is death, mourn your own, Bernado. For as surely as he is dead will you too die; or rather, you are dying; for from moment to moment your past life is dying. If it is the dead person you mourn, is it because he was bad, or because he was good? If he was bad, you are well rid of such a companion; and you should not grieve over your blessings. If he was good, which I prefer to think since he is loved by a good and prudent man, surely for him it is good to live removed from the continuous death of the body. It is not right to grudge a friend such great blessings. Perhaps you grieve because you no longer see him anywhere as you used to. However, was not this man your friend in that he loved you? Now what was it that loved you? Was it not the soul itself, the soul which also knew you? But you saw his soul no differently then than now; and you see it now no less than then.

You will perhaps complain of his absence. But, as souls do not fill space, they become present not in any particular place but in thought. When you do not consider him you cannot be sad. But when you do consider him, which you do as you please, you at once recall his presence. You should never complain about his absence then, unless perhaps you object that it is not the way of

the free soul to commune with the one now imprisoned in your
body. Separate the mind from the body, Bernado, if you can, and,
believe me, your souls will quickly meet. But if you cannot do
this, do not doubt they will meet a little later whether you will
or no. For if we compare our life to our will, it is exceedingly
brief; if we compare it to the age of the world, it is but an instant;
and, compared to the age of God, even less than an instant.

Farewell, and live in God, since He alone is eternal life. He
alone drives death and the sorrow of death far from His
worshippers.   (*Letters* 1.97)

It is not difficult to follow the steps of Ficino's reasoning,
and to see that grieving is not, in truth, reasonable, although,
of course, very understandable. But if it were possible to stand
back and let the loved one go, that would be a help for all.

In ancient India Krishna told Arjuna (who was in a difficulty not dissimilar to that of Ficino's friend Bernado):

**For those who deserve no grief thou hast grieved ... For the
living and for the dead the wise grieve not.**
                                        (*Bhagavad Gita* Ch 2 v 11)

Comfort can come from such advice and 'comfort' really
means 'with strength'. Let us therefore face the end of this
earthly life, either our own or that of others, without fear or
grieving, and with the strength of confidence in ultimate
union with God.

—XII—

What can the wise tell us with regard to our attitude to the
divine? There are supportive words from many sources to
point us to glory and happiness and abiding with God:

**Arise, shine: for thy light is come, and the glory of the Lord is
risen upon thee.**
                                        (*Isaiah* Ch 60 v 1)

Jesus said:

... If a man love me he will keep my words and my Father will love him, and we will come unto him and make our abode with him.
(*St John* Ch 14 v 23)

I am the same to all beings. I favour none, and I hate none. But those who worship Me devotedly, they live in Me and I in them.
(*Bhagavad Gita* Ch 9 v 29)

... according to Plato, true happiness is the property of the soul which, when freed from the body, contemplates the divine.
(*Letters* 1.115)

God is all about us, yet it is difficult for us to drop our personal ideas and see that this is so. For instance, we seek for happiness in this life, but then we often find it to be ephemeral. Circumstances change and the exciting pleasures of young love may end in divorce, or the joy in a new baby may be lost sight of in difficult adolescence. Plato realised that only by being freed from identification with the body or with our perceived functions and status in life, can there be unimpeded viewing of God by the soul within. This group of quotations all indicate the possibility of freedom that can come in slightly different ways, by light, love, devotion, by release from the body. We should therefore cultivate anything which leads our attention to the divine, everywhere and in every creature, and so come to that contemplation of the divine being by our true selves, free of egoism, which will lead to union with God.

—XIII—

Stillness is an essential quality in this search for freedom from fear. This can be found by resting in the Lord:

Come unto me, all ye that labour and are heavy laden, and I will give you rest. Take my yoke upon you, and learn of me; for I am meek and lowly in heart, and ye shall find rest unto your souls.
                                                    (*St Matthew* Ch 11 vv 28-29)

... since will finds rest in anything according to its measure of goodness, in infinite goodness it finds infinite rest. But if the soul, even while involved in the movement of the body, chooses the happiness that is free from all change, it will do so far more when it is beyond movement.   (*Letters* 1.115)

In both the gospel and in Ficino's letter it is clear that rest for our turbulent individual wills and wayward minds is available even while we are in this world. Ficino has used a beautiful phrase as the title of another letter on the relationships of body, mind and soul:

The soul perceives after death, and much more clearly than when in the body.   (*Letters* 1.39)

Once the soul has left the body, it will be much easier for it to turn to the infinite rest in God, free from the temptations of the world, although it can be experienced while yet in the body – if that is what we really want. The choice is ours.

—XIV—

Detachment, allowing us to see our current state of mind and heart, can also be valuable in our enquiry.

When death, which has to come to all of us, comes, all one has to keep in mind is that this body is being discarded.
                                                    (*Birth and Death* 1993)

Ficino can tell us a little more about that body and what our real essence is:

The everlasting rays of this eternal Sun are the minds of men, enveloped by the dark cloud of the body, but they turn back towards their Sun, if they will, through reason and love. Indeed, they spring back to that Sun, just as they originally sprang forth from it. Therefore, since they can flow back to their Sun at any time once all impediment has been removed by contemplating and loving rightly, they undoubtedly flowed forth from it without impediment and clearly are everlasting, being without question next to the eternal itself. They reveal their immortality most clearly when they value mortal things as nothing, especially when weighed against the eternal. Moreover, they recognise what is immortal as immortal and they realise immortality itself, that is God, through the very principle of immortality, an unshakeable proof.   (*Letters* 5.13)

How comforting to hear that we are truly shafts of light from the Sun, by which Ficino implies God. On this earth we are shrouded in the darkness that comes from our souls being encased in bodies. However, having discarded the body it seems that through reason and love we can merge with the eternal light. Thus we are immortal – part of the immortality that is God Himself. This knowledge can provide strength, particularly when this earthly life is coming to its close.

—XV—

Finally we are assured of release from the bondage of the body by words from the Bible:

He brought them out of darkness and the shadow of death, and brake their bands in sunder. (*Psalm* 107 v 14)

The psalmist sees that we can be taken from our small enclosed worlds and in particular from what we see as a looming shadow coming towards us which blights the later years of many of us. The shells in which we hide, made

entirely of our own ideas about ourselves, can be smashed and
discarded by recognition of the truth of statements like this
of the psalmist. We find ourselves in a much larger space.

This statement is echoed by Isaiah who affirms that:
'The people that walked in darkness have seen a great light'
(*Isaiah* Ch 9 v 2).

How can this recognition and release be brought about?
Not by our doings, but by realising that the eternal Spirit,
God, the absolute creative force, can make this possible
directly by grace, by letting us at last hear the truth of
words such as these in many scriptures. Thus we can come to
understand that it is possible to live in the light, perpetual
light, and when the body comes to its natural end to merge
into the eternal light, and to know that the bands that have
trapped us hitherto in the darkness can be broken and left
behind.

Then the psalmist can say with the utmost confidence:

**Return unto thy rest, O my soul; for the Lord hath dealt
bountifully with thee. For thou hast delivered my soul from
death, mine eyes from tears, and my feet from falling. I will walk
before the Lord in the land of the living ...**   (*Psalm* 116 vv 7-9)

The land of the living is where it is possible for us to be
united with God.

Chapter 5

Is there such a thing as reincarnation?

TRADITIONALLY in the West there has been the teaching that when we die we, as individuals, go to heaven or to hell, or perhaps to purgatory. In the East, however, the notion of being born again in another body is well accepted, as in the Vedantic or Buddhist traditions. Plato in ancient Greece also concluded that pre-existence of the soul and rebirth must occur, that we have been born before in other bodies. This certainly is a possibility worthy of consideration, but what have Christians thought about it?

Throughout the first 500 years or so of the Christian era, rebirth was widely accepted by many eminent saints, bishops and other Christian writers, although not by all. Later this idea was outlawed, but through the centuries some Christians have reconsidered this suggestion. Anselm, Archbishop of Canterbury, had been influenced by Plato's view on reincarnation, and in AD 1109 it is said that he pondered the origin of the soul as he lay dying. In the centuries since then, the possibility of being reborn in another body has been voiced by Christians of various denominations.

If we look carefully at some incidents recounted in the New Testament, there is evidence that in the time of Jesus there was a general acceptance of rebirth, reincarnation, pre-existence. For instance in *St Matthew* Ch 16 vv 13-14 His disciples suggested to Jesus that people were wondering if He was a reincarnation of Elias (Elijah), Jeremias (Jeremiah) or some other prophet. He didn't dismiss these suggestions about people long dead as impossible, although they did not apply to Him. Indeed after the transfiguration when Jesus is asked by the disciples about Elias, whom they had seen with Him on the mountain, Jesus says:

... Elias is come already, and they knew him not, but have done unto him whatsoever they listed. Likewise shall also the Son of man suffer of them. Then the disciples understood that He spake unto them of John the Baptist.   (*St Matthew* Ch 17 vv 12-13)

Thus Jesus Himself indicates that John the Baptist was a reincarnation of Elias, so the concept of reincarnation was clearly about at that time. There are other incidents of the same kind.

—I—

Let us begin our exploration of this aspect of death in a tradition where the idea of reincarnation is familiar:

... Everybody fears death ... but there is no such thing as death. The so-called 'death' is nothing but a natural corollary of the phenomenon of birth ... Actually the individual Self, living in the body, is immortal. It gives up an old body in order to put on a new body ...   (*Birth and Death* 1993)

A verse from the *Bhagavad Gita* has a similar thought:

Just as in this body the embodied Self passes into childhood and youth and old age, so does he pass into another body. There the wise man is not distressed.   (*Bhagavad Gita* Ch 2 v 13)

Both quotations indicate that dying is part of a natural process which must come to any creature that is born. Shri Shantananda Saraswati spells out that the Self, or Spirit that is the vital essence of each one of us, is immortal – one of the words used in speaking of eternal life. He tells us that life on earth is just an episode in eternity. Once a baby is born, so ultimately that form will die. It may be that it will die soon as a child, or it may have grown to be a woman in the prime of life, or an old man at the end of many years of service. The immortal soul may return to God when the body dies, but here this additional possibility is raised that the individual soul is born again upon the earth. As a wise Anglican clergyman once said 'There must be other classrooms'. Although it is possible for the immortal soul to drop all desires associated with earthly life, thus permitting the soul's flight back to God, that may not happen this time, and we may therefore enrol again in another classroom in this world.

—II—

This same idea is taken further in the *Bhagavad Gita*. Speaking of the Supreme Self the Lord Krishna says:

He is not born, nor does He ever die ... Unborn, eternal, unchangeable and primeval, He is not slain when the body is slain ... Just as a man casts off worn-out clothes and puts on others which are new, so the embodied Self casts off worn-out bodies and enters others which are new.

(*Bhagavad Gita* Ch 2 vv 20 and 22)

The idea of casting off a worn-out body by the inner Self or Spirit may seem strange to some of us, but perhaps if the idea of being born again is considered to be a possibility, then this statement becomes logical – if for some reason the body has become inappropriate for one's real work in life, then a

new embodiment may become necessary, one that is more
propitious to that work.

—III—

Shri Shantananda Saraswati has also said on this theme:

A man comes into existence, and goes through the modifications
of childhood, youth, adulthood and old age before he moves on
to the new form. The One, the Atman within him does not go
through any change, for it ever remains the same. The body
changes, and by association and attachment to the body the individual thinks that he himself is going through the modifications.
What is important is this: that no-one experiences birth and
death. It simply happens to be recorded by others. In reality the
Atman is neither born nor does it die, but body association
makes one feel that it does.   (*Conversations* 1982)

Have we ever considered that it is only others who witness
and record our births and our deaths, and not the individual?
Many think that when the body dies, then that is the end.
Yes, it is the end of an embodiment, but the soul, the essence
of the person, as it were, moves on together with some
characteristics of mind. As is said in the *Bhagavad Gita*:

The Spirit, which pervades all that we see, is imperishable.
Nothing can destroy the Spirit.   (*Bhagavad Gita* Ch 2 v 17)

Thus from the point of view of the individual soul at either
end of an embodiment, there is only transition, not birth
and death; only the onlooker sees a change of form. It is the
ideas in the mind that blur our vision. Let us therefore drop
such doubts so that we can see the light of God and then join
that light. Recurrent embodiments would then be at an end;
we will have become free from the cycle which begins with
birth.

If, however, we cling to some of these impurities of mind dearly loved by our egos, then those desires might well guide the soul to a new body in which they can flourish, and the cycle of lives will thus continue for a while. It is a matter of choice for us.

—IV—

From a different tradition Plato gives a view on reincarnation:

Suppose we consider the question whether the souls of men after death are or are not in the world below. There comes into my mind an ancient doctrine which affirms that they go hence into the other world, and returning hither, are born again from the dead. Now if it be true that the living come from the dead, then our souls must exist in the other world, for if not, how could they have been born again?   (*Phaedo* 70 p453)

Here Socrates reflects the view from the East, and raises the question as to whether our souls may be born again in new bodies. A little later in the same passage, he asks his disciple:

... Is there not an opposite of life, as sleep is the opposite of waking?

Agreeing, the disciple suggests death, to which Socrates replies:

And these, if they are opposites, are generated one from the other ...

He too is spelling out that once we are born we will die, but to be born in the first place we come from pre-existing life, and the sequence that follows will eventually lead to rebirth. That was understood not only by the ancient Greek and Eastern traditions, but also during the early years of the

Christian church. To step clear of this sequence is possible, as many of these quotations indicate, and thus we can return to God, our Source.

In the twentieth century Shri Shantananda Saraswati has also said:

... surrendering oneself to God removes the delusion of Maya. Then there is a dawn of true knowledge and we realise there is no death for us ...   (*Birth and Death* 1993)

—V—

And Shri Shantananda Saraswati again explores this point:

Actually there is neither birth nor death. Know that and you would be happy.   (*Birth and Death* 1993)

There is no such thing as birth and death, death is being enacted ... Birth and death relate to the body, not to the Atman ... It is the body that is born and dies. The Atman itself which inhabits the body is birthless and deathless.   (*Birth and Death* 1993)

In the *Bhagavad Gita:*

... The embodied Self in everyone's body can never be killed ... Wherefore thou oughtest not to grieve about any creature.
                              (*Bhagavad Gita* Ch 2 v 30)

These statements point out that relief comes to the mind from knowing that the cycle starting with birth does not exist in reality. If we can accept that the body, having been born will die, and that the vitality within, the soul, and parts of mind move on undying, then the next step becomes the start of a new adventure which can be seen as part of a play – a play of which we do not yet know the end.

—VI—

Finally a Christian thought on the possibility of being born
again in another body when St Paul ends an instruction about
obeying God:

**... according to the power of God; who hath saved us, and
called us with an holy calling, not according to our works, but
according to his own purpose and grace, which was given us
in Christ Jesus before the world began.**

(*Second Epistle to Timothy* Ch 1 vv 8-9)

In this personal letter to Timothy we are alerted to a very long
time span of spiritual life. In fact, it is outside time. We hear
of God's **'own purpose and grace'** provided for us **'before
the world began'**. In other words God was there prior to the
existence of the universe, and could therefore bestow grace
on us before Creation. If we have been in existence since
before time, then the likelihood that we have lived before
in other bodies must be considered as a real possibility. We
might have had a thousand bodies or more, but that which is
true and real within us is ever the same because it is a spark
of God's being within – **'according to his own purpose and
grace'**.

Having written words in tune with both Plato and the
Bhagavad Gita centuries before him, and with Shri Shantananda Saraswati in the twentieth century, centuries ahead of
him in time, St Paul, the writer of this epistle to Timothy, goes
on to say that purpose and grace are now made manifest by
Jesus Christ:

**... who hath abolished death and hath brought life and
immortality to light through the gospel.**

(*Second Epistle to Timothy* Ch 1 v 10)

If we can recognise that we are children of God, called into being by Him before Creation, then in the end there can only be everlasting light and life in God, beyond time and place.

Chapter 6

What is Life?

L IFE, ETERNAL LIFE, has already been spoken about in quotations throughout this book, but in association with other ideas. Here in this chapter responding to the sixth and last question, the quotations are primarily about life and they resound with the joy and certainty of returning to unity with God. Some speak of freedom, trust, of immortality, and first – of light, the light which illuminates the recurring question: 'Who am I?'

—I—

The Egyptian mystic Hermes Trismegistus is asked by his Mentor: '… Why does he who has remembered himself go to the Father, as the Word of God says?'

Hermes replies: 'Because the Father of all is constituted out of light and life, whence Man has been begotten.'

The Mentor then says: 'The truth is: light and life is God and Father, whence Man is begotten. If, therefore, you realise yourself as being from life and light and that you have been made out of them, you will return to life' (*The Way of Hermes* 1.21).

Many scriptures and ancient philosophies speak of light as being central to the understanding of who we really are. For instance Jesus said: 'I am the light of the world …' (*St John* Ch 8 v 12), and again:

59

Let your light so shine before men, that they may see your good works, and glorify your Father which is in heaven.

(St Matthew Ch 5 v 16)

The light that is being spoken of is the vitality, or soul, or Spirit within us, and this should not be covered or veiled in any way. It is our true nature not to hide our light, but to let that light shine and be one with God's light, to merge into His eternal light and life, and at the time of dying, or perhaps sooner, there is an opportunity for the light within each of us to merge with this, its source, if we so wish.

—II—

Similarly the *Bhagavad Gita* tells of light being the goal eternal. In the following verse the Lord Krishna speaks to Prince Arjuna of the ultimate reality:

That [the Goal], the sun illumines not, nor the moon, nor fire; That is My Supreme Abode, to which having gone none return.

(Bhagavad Gita Ch 15 v 6)

Shankara, the first Shankaracharya, explaining this verse centuries ago, wrote:

The sun, though possessed of the power of illumining all, does not illumine that Abode, the Abode of Light. That Abode to which having gone none return, and which the sun and other (luminous bodies) do not illumine, is the Highest Abode ...

(Commentary to *Bhagavad Gita* Ch 15 v 6)

This supreme abode, the abode of light, is the same light spoken of in the Christian teaching and also by Hermes, the ancient Egyptian, as described above.

—III—

What does light bring with it to help our understanding?

First St Paul urges us to: **'Put on the armour of light'** (*Epistle to the Romans* Ch 13 v 12).

Ficino adds:

And just as God has already imparted his bounteous light, so immediately he imparts life-giving warmth and joy, thus bestowing life, free from death. (*Letters* 1.39)

God has given His light to all beings; it is part of our essence giving us life in this physical world, providing strength, protection and consciousness, and thus the power to use the mind.

Can we recognise that in addition to that light, God's warmth and joy are also present? All are gifts to each one of us, His warmth in particular opening our hearts. With these blessings we can also receive the gift of life that transcends everything, and sets us free from the limitations of life on earth, and allows us full recognition of God.

—IV—

In this exploration of life we come to the word immortality, which may be described as continuity of existence; this is stressed in Vedantic teaching in ancient Indian scriptures:

Never did I not exist, nor thou ... and no-one of us will ever hereafter cease to exist. (*Bhagavad Gita* Ch 2 v 12)

Here the Lord Krishna, talking to Arjuna before a great battle, speaks with absolute certainty of the immortality of soul, of Spirit. He then says: '... **He is not slain when the body is slain**' (*Bhagavad Gita* Ch 2 v 20).

This statement is telling us that the essence of man cannot be killed, and does not and cannot die, that life itself is indestructible.

In *Isaiah* something similar is expressed: '**Incline your ear, and come unto me: hear, and your soul shall live …**' (*Isaiah* Ch 55 v 3).

So we can see the traditions of East and West agree that, if we truly hear the word of God and thus come into communion with Him, our souls will live. Each tradition expresses in its own way the same fundamental truth that there is a Supreme Being, God to whom we can return, but we need to hear what the wise are actually saying; and Jesus says '**He that hath ears to hear let him hear**' (*St Matthew* Ch 11 v 15). We need also to realise that the wise, even after many centuries, are still talking to us, now, so that we may avail ourselves of life in God.

—V—

If we take forward this idea of the immortality of the soul and its return to God, there could be true freedom, as expressed in the *Mundaka Upanishad*, where we are told of the change from life on earth to eternal life.

Those … who are assiduous and have become pure in mind through the Yoga [devotion] of monasticism – all of them, at the supreme moment of final departure, become identified with the supreme Immortality … and they become freed on every side.
(*Mundaka Upanishad* III ii 6)

By the use of the word '**monasticism**' here, the writer implies the attitude of surrender of the activities of the ego, such as was required of postulant monks by *The Rule of St Benedict* in the early sixth century AD. The letting go of 'me' and 'mine' must be allowed to happen for there to be true freedom.

The writer of the book of *Proverbs* tells us that: '**In the way of righteousness is life; and in the pathway thereof there is no death**' (*Proverbs* Ch 12 v 28).

Careful reflection is needed if we truly wish to take the conscious path of righteousness to return to God. We need to give our attention to God, learning to see Him in everyone and everything, and obeying His will and not that of the individual ego which always wants something for itself given half a chance. By this means, becoming one with the Supreme leads to freedom, and thus lasting union with God can come about – for all who want that. That would be real life.

—VI—

So what within us is everlasting, what is immortal, what truly am I? What else can shed light on this most important of questions?

How full of life is that death by which I die in myself but live in God, by which I die to the dead but live for life, and by life and rejoice in joy!   (*Letters* 1.4)

'**Die in myself**' – to what does that refer? Surely this is speaking of the little selfish self, my-self, the little 'me', the part of the mind of each of us which likes to think that it is the one all important thing in the universe. So, when it seems that life in this body will soon be over, the ego, anticipating and fearing death, can take this hard, and emotions like fear and anger may well surface.

St Paul advised the Ephesians: '**And be renewed in the Spirit of your mind**' (*Epistle to the Ephesians* Ch 4 v 23).

Shri Shantananda Saraswati speaking in recent years about man's real nature, said: '**Ego expels divinity**' (*Conversations* 1982).

These statements indicate that when our selfish natures take us over, our view shrinks and we lose sight of God and the wonderful prospect of rejoining Him; the divine within us is overshadowed, as it were, by the selfish self diverting attention on to itself. But ego is part of the mind, and mind needs to be cleansed from within, by the light of the Spirit. Let the Spirit, the inner voice of God prevail. If, as Ficino says, the individual can '**die in myself but live in God**', the whole situation can be transformed, and fear can just drop away, and we can 'rejoice in joy!'

—VII—

So it is essential to trust in the everlasting.

Thou liftest me up to the wind; thou causest me to ride upon it, and dissolvest my substance. For I know that thou wilt bring me to death, and to the house appointed for all living.

(Job Ch 30 vv 22-23)

Job speaks of complete trust in God, of allowing His will to be done, and of letting His forces guide the individual soul. Yes, He will bring us to the point of death of the body (an inevitable fact), but at that point the selfish individual nature or ego can be dissolved by God as one enters the house appointed for all true living, that is – with Him and in Him.

—VIII—

Lastly in this chapter on life, St Paul's statement of certainty that there can be no separation:

For I am persuaded, that neither death, nor life, nor angels, nor principalities, nor powers, nor things present, nor things to come, nor height, nor depth, nor any other creature, shall be able to separate us from the love of God, which is in Christ Jesus our Lord.   *(Epistle to the Romans* Ch 8 vv 38-39)

St Paul states a wide range of possible things that can get in the way of our clearly seeing God and the true workings of His wonderful universe. He tells us that not one of this array of physical and mental diversions, not even life as it is ordinarily understood, can in truth keep us from the love of God, which must, in effect, be union with Him, with truth and eternal life. This union is the true state.

Chapter 7

What the wise say
to the dying

PEOPLE WHO are dying may have lived for many years with a debilitating disease which only now seems to be bringing the end of physical life close, or they may have developed a life-threatening illness of short duration.

Whatever the circumstances, a quotation such as: '... **true happiness is the property of the soul which, when freed from the body, contemplates the divine ...**' (see Chapter 4.XII) may perhaps be seen with the eye of the mind and be heard in the heart. If the essence of this quotation is simply witnessed, any terror may be allowed to cease. Those for whom death is not imminent but is within sight (and it is within the sight of all of us), may find it useful to consider Chapter 4 on how we may turn our minds to the eternal. Can we realise our unity with God while still in our earthly bodies?

As an additional aid this chapter now provides some quotations that could be of comfort or help to those who are dying, which they might like to read for themselves. Other passages are more suitable to be read to a person in the last days or hours. So these quotations are arranged in two groups. Obviously there is some overlap, and there can be personal choice as to what seems most appropriate or appealing.

—I—
What is said by the wise directly to the dying?

DIRECT SPEECH ABOUT DEATH

Lord Krishna makes various helpful statements to Prince Arjuna:

1) ... let thy mind cling only to Me, let thy intellect abide in Me, and without doubt thou shalt live hereafter in Me alone.
(Bhagavad Gita Ch 12 v 8)

2) With the mind intent on Me ... practising Yoga [devotion], and finding refuge in Me, how in full without doubt thou shalt know Me, that do thou hear.   *(Bhagavad Gita* Ch 7 v 1)

3) I am the Self seated in the hearts of all beings. I am the beginning and the life, and I am the end of them all.
(Bhagavad Gita Ch 10 v 20)

In the same tradition, Shri Shantanada Saraswati has said:

4) Birth and death relate to the body and not to the Atman.
(Birth and Death 1993)

5) The only advice to be given at this moment is to shed all feelings of fear of going into the unknown, and remain aware that the loss of the body is not a loss in any way – you have performed the deeds which this body could have performed in the best way and there it ends.   *(Birth and Death* 1993)

6) Death does not bring an end to the one who has the body. The one who takes and discards the body is a conscious being.
(Birth and Death 1993)

Shakespeare applies reason. In his play *Measure for Measure*, advice is being given in a long speech to Claudio, a young man who has been condemned to die. He is being urged not to keep all his attention and desires on what will be lost, but to see that this outcome could bring release from the burdens of money and the fear of losing it, and the fear of leaving all other possessions behind. He is being told that – given that he has been condemned to be executed by the state – it would be a blessed release from an unbearable load, the intelligent way out of the living hell where he is completely identified with his body.

7) ... **Reason thus with life.**
      If I do lose thee, I do lose a thing
      That none but fools would keep ...
      ... Happy thou art not,
      For what thou hast not, still thou striv'st to get,
      And what thou hast, forget'st ...
      ... If thou art rich, thou'rt poor;
      For, like an ass whose back with ingots bows,
      Thou bear'st thy heavy riches but a journey,
      And death unloads thee ...

Claudio responds to this advice from the Duke (who is counselling him) by replying:

      ... I humbly thank you.
      To sue to live, I find I seek to die,
      And seeking death, find life. Let it come on.
                              (*Measure for Measure* Act III sc i from line 6)

Plato also has a direct approach:

8) SOCRATES: **Do we believe that there is such a thing as death?**
      DISCIPLE: **To be sure.**

SOCRATES: Is it not the separation of mind and body? And to be dead is the completion of this; when the soul exists in herself, and is released from the body, and the body is released from the soul, what is this but death?   (*Phaedo* 64 p447)

DIRECT SPEECH ABOUT BEING STRONG IN FAITH

The Old Testament speaks about strength in times of difficulty:

9) Have I not commanded thee? be strong and of a good courage: be not afraid, neither be thou dismayed: for the Lord thy God is with thee whithersoever thou goest.
(*Joshua* Ch 1 v 9)

10) God is our refuge and strength, a very present help in trouble. Therefore will not we fear though the earth be removed, and though the mountains be carried into the midst of the sea.   (*Psalm* 46 vv 1-2)

St Paul is also strong in faith:

11) The last enemy that shall be destroyed is death.
(*First Epistle to the Corinthians* Ch 15 v 26)

12) Stand therefore, having your loins girt about with truth, and having on the breastplate of righteousness, and your feet shod with the preparation of the gospel of peace.
(*Epistle to the Ephesians* Ch 6 vv 14-15)

DIRECT SPEECH ABOUT STILLNESS, TRUST
AND REASSURANCE

The Old Testament has much to offer:

13) The Lord bless thee and keep thee: the Lord make his face

to shine upon thee, and be gracious unto thee: the Lord lift up his countenance upon thee, and give thee peace.

(Numbers Ch 6 vv 24-26)

14) ... Behold I am with thee and will keep thee in all places whither thou goest ...   *(Genesis* Ch 28 v 15)

15) Be still and know that I am God ...   *(Psalm* 46 v 10)

16) My presence shall go with thee, and I will give thee rest.

(Exodus Ch 33 v 14)

17) ... they that dwell in the land of the shadow of death, upon them hath the light shined.   *(Isaiah* Ch 9 v 2)

18) Why art thou cast down, O my soul? and why art thou disquieted within me? Hope thou in God; for I shall yet praise him, who is the health of my countenance, and my God.

(Psalm 42 v 11)

In the Gospels:

19) I am the resurrection and the life, saith the Lord; he that believeth in me, though he were dead, yet shall he live; and whosoever liveth and believeth in me shall never die.

(St John 11 vv 25-26)

20) ... Peace, be still ...   *(St Mark* Ch 4 v 39)

St Paul's words can also help:

21) ... the law of the Spirit of life in Christ Jesus hath made me free from the law of sin and death. *(Epistle to the Romans* Ch 8 v 2)

22) When I was a child, I spake as a child, I understood as a child,

I thought as a child: but when I became a man, I put away
childish things. For now we see through a glass darkly; but then
face to face; now I know in part, but then shall I know even as
also I am known.   (*First Epistle to the Corinthians* Ch 13 vv 11-12)

In the *Bhagavad Gita* the Lord Krishna advises:

23) ... meditate always on Me ... if thy mind and thy reason
be fixed on Me, to Me shalt thou surely come.
                                        (*Bhagavad Gita* Ch 8 v 7)

DIRECT SPEECH ABOUT THE IMMORTALITY
OF THE SOUL

It can be helpful to be reminded at any time that it is only
the body that dies, and the spirit, being immortal, returns to
God:

24) That man attains peace, who, abandoning all desires, moves
about without attachment, without selfishness, without vanity.
    This is the Brahmic state ... Attaining to this, none is deluded.
Remaining in this state even at the last period of life, one attains
to the felicity of Brahman.   (*Bhagavad Gita* Ch 2 vv 71-72)

This speaks of the Spirit. Shri Shantanda Saraswati explained
verse 72 thus:

It is all-encompassing and embraces everything, having no
attachment, no sorrow, pure and peaceful, it passes into the next
world without any turmoil in its own peaceful majesty.
                                        (*Conversations* 1973)

    Lord Krishna says:

25) It [the Spirit] is named the Unmanifest, the Unthinkable,

the Immutable. Wherefore, knowing the Spirit as such, thou hast no cause to grieve.   (*Bhagavad Gita* Ch 2 v 25)

Shakespeare also recognises the mortality of the body and the return of the soul to God:

26) ... The earth can have but earth which is his due,
    My Spirit is thine, the better part of me ...   (from Sonnet 74)

—II—

Words of the wise which it may be helpful to read in the last days or hours

SOME WORDS FROM CHRISTIAN SOURCES

1) The Lord's Prayer is of comfort to many and there are numerous versions of this well known prayer; here are three:

Our Father, which art in heaven, hallowed be thy Name. Thy kingdom come. Thy will be done in earth as it is in heaven. Give us this day our daily bread. And forgive us our trespasses, as we forgive them that trespass against us. And lead us not into temptation; but deliver us from evil: for thine is the kingdom, the power and the glory, for ever and ever. Amen.
                    (*Book of Common Prayer*)

... Our Father which art in heaven, hallowed be thy name. Thy kingdom come. Thy will be done in earth, as it is in heaven. Give us this day our daily bread. And forgive us our debts, as we forgive our debtors. And lead us not into temptation, but deliver us from evil: for thine is the kingdom, and the power, and the glory, for ever.   (*St Matthew* Ch 6 vv 9-13)

... Our Father which art in heaven, hallowed be Thy name. Thy kingdom come. Thy will be done, as in heaven, so in earth. Give us day by day our daily bread. And forgive us our sins; for we also forgive every one that is indebted to us. And lead us not into temptation; but deliver us from evil.

(*St Luke* Ch 11 vv 2-4)

2) The following words of Zacharias are well known to users of the *Book of Common Prayer* where the passage is known as Benedictus. They are the first words of Zacharias after speech was restored to him following the birth of his son, John the Baptist:

And thou, child, shalt be called the prophet of the Highest: for thou shalt go before the face of the Lord to prepare his ways;to give knowledge of salvation unto his people for the remission of their sins, through the tender mercy of our God: whereby the day-spring from on high hath visited us; to give light to them that sit in darkness, and in the shadow of death, and to guide our feet into the way of peace.   (*St Luke* Ch 1 vv 76-79)

3) Words of the aged Simeon blessing the infant Jesus in the Temple, are also known as the Nunc Dimitis:

Lord now lettest thou thy servant depart in peace, according to thy word: for mine eyes have seen thy salvation, which thou hast prepared before the face of all people; a light to lighten the Gentiles and the glory of thy people Israel. (*St Luke* Ch 2 vv 29-32)

4) In the beginning was the Word, and the Word was with God and the Word was God.
The same was in the beginning with God.
All things were made by him; and without him was not any thing made that was made.
In him was life, and the life was the light of men.

And the light shineth in darkness; and the darkness compre-
hended it not.

There was a man sent from God, whose name was John.

The same came for a witness, to bear witness of the Light, that
all men through him might believe.

He was not that Light, but was sent to bear witness of that
Light.

That was the true Light, which lighteth every man that cometh
into the world.

He was in the world, and the world was made by him, and the
world knew him not.

He came unto his own, and his own received him not.

But as many as received him, to them gave he power to
become the sons of God, even to them that believe on his
name:

Which were born, not of blood, nor of the will of the flesh, nor
of the will of man, but of God.

And the Word was made flesh, and dwelt among us, (and we
beheld his glory, the glory as of the only begotten of the
Father) full of grace and truth.   (*St John* Ch 1 vv 1-14)

5) Now unto him that is able to do exceedingly abundantly above
all that we ask or think, according to the power that worketh
in us, unto him be the glory in the church by Christ Jesus
throughout all ages, world without end. Amen.

(*Epistle to the Ephesians* Ch 3 v 20)

6) ... Mercy unto you and peace and love be multiplied ...

(*Epistle of St Jude* v 2)

FROM THE BOOK OF COMMON PRAYER

Some of the collects and special prayers designated for use on
certain days in the Church's calendar or at particular services,
can also be of value at this time:

A collect that speaks of peace and lack of fear:

7) O God, from whom all holy desires, all good counsels, and all just works do proceed; Give unto thy servants that peace which the world cannot give; that both our hearts may be set to obey thy commandments, and also that by thee we being defended from the fear of our enemies may pass our time in rest and quietness; through the merits of Jesus Christ our Saviour. Amen.

(Second Collect at Evening Prayer)

The following collects speak of transcending death:

8) Almighty God, who through thy only-begotten Son Jesus Christ hast overcome death, and opened unto us the gate of everlasting life; We humbly beseech thee, that, as by thy special grace preventing us thou dost put into our minds good desires, so by thy continual help we may bring the same to good effect; through Jesus Christ our Lord, who liveth and reigneth with thee and the Holy Ghost, ever one God, world without end. Amen.

(Collect for the Tuesday in Easter-week)

9) Grant, we beseech thee, Almighty God, that like as we do believe thy only-begotten Son our Lord Jesus Christ to have ascended into the heavens; so we may also in heart and mind thither ascend, and with him continually dwell, who liveth and reigneth with thee and the Holy Ghost, one God, world without end. Amen.

(Collect for Ascension Day)

10) O God, the protector of all that trust in thee, without whom nothing is strong, nothing is holy; Increase and multiply upon us thy mercy; that, thou being our ruler and guide, we may so pass through things temporal, that we finally lose not the things eternal: Grant this, O heavenly Father, for Jesus Christ's sake our Lord. Amen.

(Collect for the Fourth Sunday after Trinity Sunday)

11) O God, who hast prepared for them that love thee such good things as pass man's understanding; Pour into our hearts such love toward thee, that we, loving thee above all things, may obtain thy promises, which exceed all that we can desire; through Jesus Christ our Lord. Amen.

(Collect for the Sixth Sunday after Trinity Sunday)

A group of collects that speak of help and direction:

12) O Lord, we beseech thee mercifully to hear us; and grant that we, to whom thou hast given an hearty desire to pray, may by thy mighty aid be defended and comforted in all dangers and adversities, through Jesus Christ our Lord. Amen.

(Collect for the Third Sunday after Trinity Sunday)

13) O God, forasmuch as without thee we are not able to please thee; mercifully grant, that thy Holy Spirit may in all things direct and rule our hearts; through Jesus Christ our Lord. Amen.

(Collect for the Nineteenth Sunday after Trinity Sunday)

14) O Almighty and most merciful God, of thy bountiful good-ness keep us, we beseech thee, from all things that may hurt us; that we, being ready both in body and soul, may cheerfully accomplish those things that thou wouldst have done; through Jesus Christ our Lord. Amen.

(Collect for the Twentieth Sunday after Trinity Sunday)

15) God, who as at this time didst teach the hearts of thy faithful people, by the sending to them the light of thy Holy Spirit: grant us by the same Spirit to have a right judgement in all things, and evermore to rejoice in His holy comfort; through the merits of Christ Jesus our Saviour, who liveth and reigneth with thee in the unity of the same Spirit, one God, world without end. Amen.

(Collect for the Monday in Whitsun week)

Some collects and blessings that could be a preparation for
what is to come:

16) **Grant, we beseech thee, merciful Lord, to thy faithful
people pardon and peace, that they may be cleansed from
all their sins, and serve thee with a quiet mind; through Jesus
Christ our Lord. Amen.**

(Collect for the Twenty-first Sunday after Trinity Sunday)

17) **Almighty God, unto whom all hearts be open, all desires
known, and from whom no secrets are hid; cleanse the thoughts
of our hearts by the inspiration of thy Holy Spirit, that we may
perfectly love thee, and worthily magnify thy holy Name; through
Christ our Lord. Amen.**
(Collect from the Communion Service, in the *Book of Common Prayer*)

18) **The peace of God, which passeth all understanding, keep
your hearts and minds in the knowledge and love of God, and of
His son Jesus Christ our Lord: and the blessing of God Almighty,
the Father, the Son, and the Holy Ghost, be amongst you and
remain with you always. Amen.**   (The blessing at the end of the
Communion Service in the *Book of Common Prayer*)

19) **Unto God's gracious mercy and protection we commit
thee. The Lord bless thee and keep thee. The Lord make his
face to shine upon thee, and be gracious unto thee. The Lord lift
up his countenance upon thee and give thee peace, both now
and evermore. Amen.**
(From the Visitation of the Sick in the *Book of Common Prayer*)

WORDS FROM THE OLD TESTAMENT OF THE BIBLE

20) Psalm 23. Here are two versions of this well known psalm,
one from the Bible and the second from the *Book of Common
Prayer*:

The Lord is my shepherd; I shall not want.

He maketh me to lie down in green pastures: he leadeth me beside the still waters.

He restoreth my soul: he leadeth me in the paths of righteousness for his name's sake.

Yea, though I walk through the valley of the shadow of death, I will fear no evil: for thou art with me; thy rod and thy staff they comfort me.

Thou preparest a table before me in the presence of mine enemies: thou anointest my head with oil; my cup runneth over.

Surely goodness and mercy shall follow me all the days of my life: and I will dwell in the house of the Lord for ever.

(Psalm 23)

The Lord is my shepherd: therefore can I lack nothing.

He shall feed me in a green pasture: and lead me forth beside the waters of comfort.

He shall convert my soul: and bring me forth in the paths of righteousness, for his Name's sake.

Yea, though I walk through the valley of the shadow of death, I will fear no evil: for thou art with me; thy rod and thy staff comfort me.

Thou shalt prepare a table before me against them that trouble me: thou hast anointed my head with oil, and my cup shall be full.

But thy loving-kindness and mercy shall follow me all the days of my life: and I will dwell in the house of the Lord for ever.

(Book of Common Prayer)

WORDS FROM THE *BHAGAVAD GITA*

21) I am the Father of the universe and its Mother; I am its Nourisher and its Grandfather; I am the Knowable and the Pure; I am Om; I am the Sacred Scriptures.

I am the Goal, the Sustainer, the Lord, the Witness, the Home,
the Shelter, the Lover and the Origin; I am Life and Death;
I am the Fountain and the Seed Imperishable.
I am the Heat of the Sun. I release and hold back the Rains. I am
Death and Immortality. I am Being and Not-Being.

(Ch 9 vv 17-19)

22) I am the source of all; from Me everything evolves; thus
thinking, the wise worship Me, endowed with contemplation.
With their thought on Me, with their life absorbed in me,
instructing each other, and ever speaking of Me, they are
content and delighted.
To these, ever devout, worshipping Me with love, I give that
devotion of knowledge by which they come to Me.
Out of mere compassion for them, I, abiding in their self, destroy
the darkness born of ignorance, by the luminous lamp of
wisdom. (Ch 10 vv 8-11)

23) As the mighty wind, though moving everywhere, has no
resting place but space, so have all these beings no home but
Me. (Ch 9 v 6)

WORDS FROM THE *BRIHADARANYKA UPANISHAD*

24) A prayer that is familiar in English, but which originally
comes from this Upanisad:

From untruth lead me to Truth; From darkness lead me to Light;
From death lead me to Immortality.

(*Brihadaranyaka Upanishad* 1.3.28)

Chapter 8

Advice and help for the bereaved from the words of the wise

T HE WORD 'bereaved' comes from an Old English word meaning 'to plunder'. A person bereaved feels that he has been robbed of husband, mother, son or some other to whom there is deep attachment. This is a recognisable state which all can understand. That attachment may, to some extent, be to the physical form of the one who has died. Thus this sense of being robbed is associated with a claim on that person, who was 'my' daughter, 'my' father and so on. In this state there is vulnerability, and often a great desire to be re-united with that physical form again in heaven. As is stated in Chapter 4.X '… **it is very difficult for people to transcend the love of the physical body** …' Both mind and heart become limited by these feelings. Fear will also come into the mind – fears for the future, of not meeting again, also fear concerning one's own mortality, of guilt, regret, and many more. The power of these fears, as is described in the introduction, takes many forms.

In this book, wisdom concerning the subject usually known as death has been assembled from writings in many centuries and traditions. What is demonstrated in the extracts is, firstly, the fact that this fear has disturbed the minds of people all through the ages, and further, that the wise throughout history have turned their attention to helping others through such troubled times. Thus we are not alone in bereavement. These quotations face some of the fears suffered by those of us who are grieving, and if it may be possible for some of us to make use of one or more passages to alleviate individual troubles, then the view may broaden, the perception change and rejoicing for the one who has died may become possible, and so darkness can be replaced by light. To celebrate the life of such a one publicly, perhaps at a memorial service, and/or by happy recollections intertwined with everyday life, can help enormously during the necessary and inevitable period of adjustment known as bereavement.

Marsilio Ficino's wonderful letter to a grieving friend (Chapter 4.XI) sets out the path of reason to help cope with the apparently missing loved one. However, not everyone can respond to reason at such an emotional time when the main cause of distress may well be, for instance, guilt at things said or left unsaid. Even the clear statement, '... **there is no such thing as death. The so-called "death" is nothing but a natural corollary of the phenomenon of birth**' (See Chapter 5.I), may not be heard and appreciated; after all it is a rather unfamiliar view.

Perhaps if the mind can be allowed to fill with words such as those of Jesus: '**Peace I leave with you, my peace I give unto you: not as the world giveth, give I unto you. Let not your heart be troubled, neither let it be afraid**' (*St John* Ch 14. v 27), then light could come, and with such light and the certainty of the love of God, it can become possible to accept the fact that while the natural consequence of birth is for the body ultimately to die, the soul, the essence of the person, is then free to return to unity with God.

The physical state of the loved one prior to death will undoubtedly have a bearing on the feelings of those who were nearest to that person. There is likely to be a difference in those feelings towards an elderly friend or relative who has had a long and painful illness and a child or young adult struck down suddenly. Perceptions and effects will vary for a host of reasons. Remembering that once a being is born, that body will ultimately die, a wise course of action is '... **cherishing the divine and disregarding the mortal**' (Chapter 4.I), difficult though that may be.

All of us are approaching bodily death, and although this fact is not usually appreciated by those under the age of about 60, it is nevertheless true – the body is not immortal. So it would be useful and practical for all of us to accept that fact, and then to seek to enter into communion with God during our time on earth, and to help others to do so. If this can happen, then when the time comes there will arise certain knowledge that the soul, which is immortal, can return to God or at least to come closer to Him.

Ficino says:

But if the soul, even while involved in the movement of the body chooses the happiness that is free from all change, it will do so far more when it is beyond movement.   (See Chapter 4.XIII)

To be free from that which constantly changes, is freedom indeed.

Sources and Glossary

Selection of main sources

When considering which sources of wisdom should be explored for use in this study, it was decided that they must span many centuries and include varied cultures. Also, for practical reasons, it seemed sensible to start with works fairly familiar to the compiler. But a year's search of these sources produced such rich findings that it was clearly time to share what had already been found, rather than to continue exploration of the literature.

The sources chosen therefore, in addition to the Bible which had been widely studied in schooldays, were the words of the following: William Shakespeare, Plato, some ancient Sanskrit texts from India, Hermes Trismegistus from Egypt, the extensive correspondence of Marsilio Ficino – a priest and neo-Platonist in 15th-century Florence, and most recently the words of Shri Shantanada Saraswati, the Shankaracharya of the North in India, a teacher of the Vedantic tradition in the 20th century.

Method of selection of extracts

This occurred in three phases:

Firstly: there was selection of a wide range of passages relevant in some way to death, to the soul, and to what might happen after death. This was guided partly by memory followed by verification, and partly by pursuing a particular theme with the aid of a concordance or an index to an individual book.

Secondly: this material was sifted slowly with a quiet mind, with reflection on the relevance to the aim of this project, some extracts being found to resonate with others, leading to a useful sequence; others did not and were set aside for possible use later. This phase blended into the next.

Thirdly: there was gradual realisation of how the selected quotations could be assembled and linked to provide a continuous narrative that might be of practical use.

Sources

As the selected works and authors may be unfamiliar to some who pick up this book, notes are provided to help readers who have not yet found their way to this type of literature.

A short glossary follows of words that may be confusing or unknown.

Apocrypha

The name given to certain books included at the end of some versions of the Old Testament of the Bible (see below), but which are not accepted by all as scripture.

Bhagavad Gita

The most spiritual and important part of a much larger work called the *Mahabharata* written in Sanskrit. Its date is disputed by scholars, with 3500 BC, 1500 BC and 200 BC all being considered possible by various authorities. The *Bhagavad Gita* recounts a conversation between Krishna, an incarnation of the god Vishnu, and the Prince Arjuna, on a battlefield just before the start of a civil war. Arjuna is a warrior who does not wish to take part in this war against part of his own family. Krishna speaks to him in this work of 700 verses, of devotion and duty, the giving up of attachments, of renunciation, thus giving him the spiritual nourishment he needed. This nourishment is still available and valuable today in day to day living.

The Bible

A library of books divided into two main parts:

THE OLD TESTAMENT

This contains a wide variety of Jewish history and literature, written by many different people over about 1000 years. It affirms faith, recounts the story of the Jews from the time of Abraham, through the exile in Egypt, the escape to the wilderness and the return to the Promised Land. The authorship of this part, the Pentateuch, was attributed to Moses but was written by five different authors between 1150 and 400 BC. It starts with the well-known story of the creation and of Adam and Eve in the book of *Genesis*. Historical books written by prophets and scribes, perhaps as early as 1430 BC, tell of the often turbulent history of the Jews in the land of Israel, including the acquisition of a king, Saul, and subsequent kings such as David (1010-970 BC) and Solomon.

In due course most of the Jews, having been overcome by warlike neighbours, were exiled to Babylon in about 570 BC. Several priests and prophets tell this part of the story in vivid language, and of the eventual return of many Jews to Jerusalem. Some of these later writings are told in the *Apocrypha* (see above).

The Jewish version of this collection of books differs at times from the Old Testament as used by Christians.

The Old Testament also includes some beautiful poetry, notably the *Psalms*, words of wisdom found in the book of *Proverbs*, and touching and salutary stories of individuals like Job. Some of the later books are personal statements by prophets and others, including Isaiah, Hosea and Ezekiel.

Quotations selected for this book from the Old Testament, come from the *Psalms*, the book of *Proverbs*, some of the prophetic works, as well as from the historical books and earlier times.

The Old Testament is a wonderful statement of the Law and the Prophets (of which Jesus Christ speaks) which is very important in Christian eyes, but is overtaken in importance for them by the New Testament.

THE NEW TESTAMENT

This is the foundation of Christianity, the religion that arose out of Judaism after the crucifixion and the rising from the dead of Jesus Christ, Son of God. His story is told in the four gospels, *St Matthew, St Mark, St Luke* and *St John*. The first three gospels contain many of the same words, teachings, parables and miracles of Jesus, but in each gospel there is specific material found in it alone. The gospel of *St John* differs from the first three, omitting much that they use, and including a great deal more of the words of Jesus. All four contain accounts of the betrayal and death of Christ.

The next book, the *Acts of the Apostles*, recounts the ascension of Jesus into heaven and the coming of the Holy Spirit to His followers which enabled them to preach in His name and thus lay the foundations of Christianity. This book also tells of the conversion of St Paul from being a persecutor of Christians into an inspired missionary, who took the teaching of and about Christ to the world outside Jewry. Christian teachings are also spelled out in different ways in the many letters (epistles) that he wrote to the scattered communities of Christians around the Mediterranean. Other epistles by other disciples are also found in the New Testament; and the last book is the apocalyptic *Revelation of St John*.

The statements selected from the New Testament for this book are largely the words of Jesus, with extracts from some of the epistles.

Book of Common Prayer (1662)
The prayer book of the Church of England and of the Anglican Communion worldwide for over 300 years, was largely prepared by Thomas

Cranmer (Archbishop of Canterbury from 1533 to 1556), and modified slightly over the next century. Many of the prayers were written by Cranmer, and some of these are included in Chapter 7. In recent years this prayer book has, to a great extent, been superseded.

Ficino, Marsilio (1433-1499)
Son of the physician to Cosimo de Medici in Florence, Ficino's considerable talents were recognised at an early age by Cosimo. Ficino trained as a doctor, became a philosopher, a musician and later a priest. Among many great achievements he, following Cosimo's instructions, translated from Greek into Latin the recently rediscovered works of Plato, Hermes Trismegistus, and others so that they could be appreciated in the West. Ficino also wrote commentaries on them. Following Cosimo's direction he became leader of the Platonic Academy, a jewel of the Renaissance, seeking to harmonise the teachings of Plato with those of Christianity. In addition he carried on a wide and profound correspondence with many influential people not only in Italy, but in other countries including Hungary, Germany, France and England, where he wrote to John Colet, Dean of St Paul's.

Hermes Trismegistus
An ancient Egyptian sage about whom little is known. There is doubt as to when he lived, but it seems possible that he was a contemporary of Moses, a view that Ficino shared; however he may have lived later. His 14 treatises under the title *The Way of Hermes* indicate influences from Judaic teachings, the Stoics, and Plato. These writings, in Greek, reached the West in the 15th century AD, and greatly affected philosophical thought in the Florentine Renaissance.

Plato (428-348 BC)
An aristocratic Athenian, Plato was influenced by Socrates into accepting philosophy as a way of life, and the vital importance of wisdom and reason. After Socrates' death he travelled widely, eventually returning to Athens to found his Academy for the study of Philosophy, Mathematics and Science. He wrote some 20 philosophical dialogues portraying Socrates in profound discussion with others on a variety of topics. These masterpieces have survived the centuries, having been translated many times.

Shankara
This great sage was born into a Brahmin family in Southern India. Again scholars are not agreed as to when he lived, suggestions being as far apart

as 500 BC and 700 AD, the former date being more likely. He devoted himself to spiritual work at an early age, travelling widely in India, preaching the unity of existence and the immortality of the soul, and debating with and inspiring many at a time when religious values were in decline. He also founded four important monasteries in the north, south, east and west of India, each with its own leader or teacher, now called Shankaracharya or the teacher of Shankara's philosophy, and these foundations survive to this day. In addition to writing several original spiritual works, he wrote commentaries of great profundity on many important Sanskrit scriptures such as the *Upanishads* and the *Bhagavad Gita*. He died aged only 32.

Shri Shantanada Saraswati
He held the position of Shankaracharya of the North at Jyoti Math in India from 1952 to 1980. A man of great wisdom, he was an exponent of Vedantic philosophy, helping countless people from all over the world who were seeking spiritual guidance, regardless of their faith . Quotations used are drawn from two primary sources, namely conversations that he held with Dr Francis Roles, and with Mr Leon MacLaren. He died in 1997.

Shakespeare, William
Born in Stratford-on-Avon, England in 1564. He died in 1616.

He is well known as a poet and playwright of power and perception, with plays still in production all over the world. While there is much appreciation of his superb command of language and stagecraft, his insights into philosophy and his depth of thought are not always fully acknowledged. In the sonnets there is often reference to God and the soul, rather than to other human beings.

Socrates (469-399 BC)
A soldier in his early years, he turned to philosophy, conducting public discussions on ethical matters, seeking to reveal truth. He wrote nothing, and he said that he knew nothing, but his teachings are known to us through the writings of Plato.

Upanishads
These are a series of philosophical writings in Sanskrit, from India, and they aim to dispel ignorance by revealing knowledge of the Supreme Spirit.The two Upanishads which are quoted from in this book are the Brihadaranyka Upanisad written down probably in about 800 BC, or perhaps much earlier, and the Mundaka Upanisad written down at the latest in about 400 BC; once again opinions of scholars vary.

Glossary

Absolute   A word used in Vedantic writings to represent the Supreme Absolute Being.

Atman   The Spirit of God within an individual. It is birthless and deathless.

Brahman   The Supreme Spirit, God, the Absolute power from whom the Creation comes.

Immortality   Survival of the essence of one's being beyond the death of the physical body.

Maya   The illusion of a Creation separate from its Creator, God, and equated by Shankara with ignorance, because, due to its multifarious appearances, it obscures the knowledge of unity of all Creation with the one God.

Philosophy   Literally means love of wisdom. Currently it has come to mean what an individual thinks about a subject, such as life. In this book it is used in the older sense of pursuing wisdom and knowledge for love of them alone.

Prevent   In the collect (7.II.8) this word is used in the old sense of 'to precede'.

Religion   A system of belief in, of recognition of, or an awakened sense of a higher unseen controlling power. Religions seem to vary to suit different minds and ways of understanding, each expressing truth in its own way.

Scripture   Literally something written; the sacred writings of a religion.

Self   When written as 'Self' in Vedantic literature this indicates the Absolute, the Supreme Being. But when written as 'self' it is speaking of the individual, the ego.

Soul   The innermost being or nature, the essence or indwelling or animating principle of an individual. Writers often use the word 'soul', and although there is some variation in the meaning of this word over the centuries, it seems that it is often synonymous with Spirit, and so in this book it has been considered in that sense – the essence of a being.

Spirit   The vital principle of a being, the life, the principle of thought, animation, real meaning, essence, the soul. From a Latin word meaning 'breathe'.

Vedanta   Teaching that puts forward the views that there is only one Self or Absolute Being. Within this Being there is unity of Creation in countless forms. It speaks of the divinity of the soul, and of harmony of all religions.

Wisdom   The quality of being wise; the ability to make right use of knowledge; spiritual perception. In the *Apocrypha* wisdom is given many attributes:

> ... in her is an understanding spirit, holy, one only ... lively, clear, undefiled, not subject to hurt, loving the thing that is good ... kind to man ... sure, free from care, having all power, overseeing all things, and going through all understanding, pure ... She passeth and goeth through all things by reason of her pureness. For she is the breath of the power of God and a pure influence flowing from the glory of the Almighty ... For she is the brightness of the everlasting light, the unspotted mirror of the power of God, and the image of His goodness. And being but one she can do all things and remaining in herself, she maketh all things new; and in all ages entering into holy souls she maketh them friends of God ... For she is more beautiful than the sun, and above all the order of the stars; being compared with the light she is found before it.

> *(Wisdom of Solomon Ch 7 vv 22-29)*

Wise   Having knowledge and being able to make good use of it, dictated by wisdom (see above).

Yoga   This is a Sanskrit word derived from the basic meaning to join. It is commonly used in the sense of devotion and unity.

Index of Quotations

Acknowledgements

FIRST TO Mr David Boddy who instigated this study, and whose encouragement sustained its progress. Second to the ladies who kindly read much of the text in draft form and made many helpful comments: friends Dorothy Boux, Helen Harper, Claire McCall, Jo Reeves, Jean Shepherd, Elizabeth Ward, and my late sister Diana Seward. And to many others: those who provided an occasional insight or fact, those whose kind enquiries as to progress helped the development of the work, and to my publisher Anthony Werner and my editor Margaret Colwell, whose skill and deep knowledge of the subject has proved invaluable.

Permission from the following to include copyright works is gratefully acknowledged:

Extracts from the Authorized Version of The Bible (King James Bible), the rights to which are vested in the Crown, are reproduced with permission of the Crown's Patentee, Cambridge University Press

Extracts from *The Book of Common Prayer*, the rights to which are vested in the Crown, are reproduced with permission of the Crown's Patentee, Cambridge University Press

Extracts from *The Way of Hermes*, translated by Clement Salaman *et al*, by permission of Gerald Duckworth & Co Ltd

Extracts from *Mundaka Upanishad*, translated by Swami Gambhirananda, and from *Brihadaranyaka Upanishad*, translated by Swami Madhavananda, by permission of Advaita Ashrama

Extracts from the *Bhagavad Gita*, translated by Alladi Mahadeva Sastry, by permission of Samata Books

Extracts from *The Letters of Marsilio Ficino*, translated by members of the Language Department of the School of Economic Science, by permission of Shepheard-Walwyn (Publishers) Ltd

Extracts from *Birth and Death*, sayings of Shri Shantananda Saraswati, by permission of the Study Society

Extracts from *Conversations* between Shri Shantananda Saraswati and Leon MacLaren, by permission of the School of Economic Science